Let Di Song Of Change Blow Over My Head

**Thanks and love
as always to my family
and friends.**

**If you would like to visit
di Facebook island, go to
www.facebook.com/livelikeajimmybuffettsong**

Chapter 1
"It's those changes in islanditude."

I awakened from my nightly voyage to another day, and opened my eyes. And as usual, it was as if someone had placed a beautiful, thoughtful, surprise gift in front of me. Or in this case, all around me.

There's nothing quite so fine as waking up close to Mother Ocean, near enough so you can smell and hear her. The sensation makes you *want* to lift those eyelids, so your orbs can join in the joy your nose and ears are already partaking of. And how you start your morning is half the battle; if you begin it somewhere high above sea level, you save yourself a lot of climbing to try and reach that elusive good day hiding amongst all the storm clouds.

My name is Jack Danielson, and I've been spending a lot of time lately up where the air is thin enough to make you feel giddy.

The cockatoo that lived near my hut was the only thing close to an alarm I heard these days. My morning tended to start fashionably late, and there wasn't much left of it before it metamorphosed into an afternoon. But the real change was not minding facing consciousness, and actually looking forward to it. There was a time I didn't know that was possible, and it shows how screwed up life can get, when living it is something we almost dread. Not wishing you could sleep through it all is the only way to fly.

My little shack on the beach had evolved somewhat over the last year. Gone was my hammock, or moved at least, to an outdoor location for long afternoon naps and beach party pass outs. In its place and beneath me as I lay drinking in my morning ambiance was a simple bed, an upgrade I'd relented to when I found that sleeping in the shape of a banana every evening was causing me pain, the like of which I hadn't felt since playing pinata to a Peterbilt's stick. Not to mention that while making love in a hammock is an interesting experience to try, it's also a dangerous one, and I'd grown tired of wasting half my attention on balance when there were so many other more useful and delightful things to focus on instead.

Not that it mattered though, at least for the time being. My Isabella was gone, having left di island to marry an insurance tycoon from upstate Connecticut. To add insult to injury, she'd met him on one of her visits to *my* Key West, which I'd instigated to begin with. I suppose uncle Billy Black Dog was right; she probably had been too much woman for me, or at least she wanted more than what I was willing to give her, which didn't include a big house in America. So Isabella and I ended up being the quintessential two ships passing in the night, I on my way to di island,

and she sailing away from it. When she left me, or more accurately failed to come back to me from the Keys, it felt as if a pirate cutlass had been thrust through my heart, but I wouldn't have given up a single moment of our time to ease the pain. It'd been a helluva lot of fun while our two boats had been lashed together, and I wished her all the happiness she can find.

I got up off my rack and padded across the wood floor and out of the bedroom, which would have been difficult a few months back since there used to be only one room in my thatched castle. But having Jedidiah and some of di other islanders build me a decent sized add on afforded me the space for a basic kitchen, and more importantly, an area large enough to continue the festivities out of the rain whenever Mother Nature decided to put out the beach fire during one of my luaus. And the electricity that now powered my Buffett and Marley tunes, and recharged my Margaritaville Frozen Concoction Maker, was a welcome addition, too. Not to mention my lovely little outhouse retreat.

Straight up Robinson Crusoeing it had been great fun for a while. But it turned out there were a certain number of necessities a Jack Danielson needs to be truly content, and eventually I'd found I could have my Key Lime pie and eat it too. I still lived on the beach, and there was still a thatched roof above my head. I just spent less time squatting in the bushes and more time washing mangoes and papayas in the sink before blending them with my Captain Billy's rum.

Life on di island was good, and other than Isabella's sudden departure and my few baby steps back towards civilization, hadn't changed much lately. The days still floated by like the waters of a river, seemingly coming and going at the same time. There were ups and downs, but the downs were more like gentle valleys as opposed to the deep, gaping canyons of my old life as an Image Maker public relations lackey. Even the ups were often hard to discern; not because I didn't have any great days, but because my mood lived at a higher altitude now to begin with. It was difficult to make out one mountain top from the rest, unless you count the volcanic activity that had been Isabella. And as I said, that lava had flowed.

So I just kept living my song, bobbing along on the tide like a buoy, sometimes wondering if there was ever again going to be something that would make my warning bell ring. I don't know if we ever lose the feeling once we've had it that the other flip-flop is about to drop. Paranoia is embedded deep within most of we modern natives of civilized Earth, and all the relaxing on the beach isn't going to change that. And usually for good reason, since the rest of the civilized world has a way of finding us no matter how far we fly from the nest, bringing with it all the things we've tried to leave behind.

Even when the place you've flown to is as far away as di island.

Chapter 2
"Di weather girl's here, I hope she'll be beautiful."

I walked out my front door onto one of my favorite places in the world, my porch. I was planning to plop down on my bench, watch the sand and water peacefully trade territory, and work my way towards working my way towards the rum factory. But I spied Boyd's little skiff out tooling around in the water, and walked across the beach towards he and the shoreline.

"Ahoy!" I shouted.

Boyd looked around, his long hair blowing in the late morning breeze. "Ahoy back at'cha!" he yelled.

"Any luck today?" I asked.

"A couple, so far," said Boyd. "A decent start; I was thinking of taking a break. Course, I'm always thinking of taking a break."

"Come in to shore, if you like," I said.

"I will," said Boyd, and he pointed the rudder at me.

Boyd had a couple of new sidelines to go along with being the caretaker of di island's tiny cemetery. He now spent many of his mornings diving in search of conch, some of which he sold to the Innkeeper, and to Geeah and Terrance at the Cantina. But the bulk of his molluscus treasure was purchased by Henri D. Robichaux, a relative newcomer to di island.

Henri, like Boyd, was from N'awleans. He told me the night we'd met at Monkey Drool's that he was of Cajun descent; or Creole. I was pretty sure it was one of those two, but I couldn't quite remember which, because he'd introduced himself the night the Innkeeper had unveiled his latest concoction, the Toasted Toucan. All things considered, it was a wonder I didn't think he was Mongolian.

Henri ran Robichaux's, a small cafe restaurant recently built on the beach roughly midway between the southern docks and the Monkey. It was a nice, rough wood place, with a big deck overlooking the water, providing a perfect vantage point for Henri's sunrise breakfasts. The food was excellent, a delicious mixture of Cajun (or Creole) and Caribbean seafood dishes, and when you topped it all off with the foot stomping fiddle playing of Henri's cousin Michel, who had joined him on di island, you could definitely *laissez les bons temps rouler* (let the good times roll).

Henri was an accomplished saucier who'd grown tired of waiting for a chance at wearing zee head chef hat, and had come to di island to open his own gastronomical outpost. It seemed like an odd place on this big ol' world to choose to attempt such a venture, but since I'd decided to try and run a rum

11

factory on the same little archipelago, I wasn't gonna be the one to try and talk him out of it.

And anyway, it was Boyd who'd suggested di island to Henri as a possible place for the restaurant to begin with. The two had met back in N'awleans where Boyd used to wash Henri's sauce pans, and they'd stayed in touch by carrier seagull or message in a bottle ever since. Boyd now put in the occasional shift at the new island restaurant as well, filling in wherever Henri needed him. Which seemed to be more and more often, as the popularity of the place grew, much to the Innkeeper's chagrin.

Boyd dropped his anchor a short distance from shore, and waded through the shallow water onto the beach. I'd loped into my hut to grab a couple of bottles of papaya juice I kept stored in my small refrigerator, now that I had one, and gave one to Boyd when he reached land.

"How goes the morning?" said Boyd, as we sat down in the shade of the palm trees on chairs around my fire pit.

"I'm still breathing in and breathing out," I said. "And I still haven't found any reason to move on. And you? Anything new on the Coconut Telegraph?"

"Not much to pass on," said Boyd. "Gus flew in this morning."

I would have looked at my watch, if I'd owned one that I hadn't already chucked into the ocean. Instead I looked up at the sky. "Already? It can't be past noon yet, is it?"

"No, although it's getting close," said Boyd.

"That's about the third time this week he's been early; he must be slipping," I said.

"Ever since Jolly Roger started running his passenger route to Tortola on the Crustacean II, Gus has been forced to fly in the AM more and more often to get his piece of all the new travelers," said Boyd.

"I bet that's making him happy," I said.

"Yeah, he's been in a pretty pissy mood lately," said Boyd. "Even for Gus, that is."

In the old days, if someone had wanted to travel to di island, they likely would have looked up surly pilot Gus Grizwood and his old wooden Noorduyn Norseman seaplane, *The Painkiller.* At the time, he was the only one flying out to us on a fairly regular basis, and only in the afternoons, since mornings would have cut down drastically on his recovery time from lengthy Soggy Dollar sessions. But since the rum factory opened there were more and more Virgin Island vacationers who wanted to visit for tours, while the growing population of di islanders wanted to go back the other way for shopping.

So our own smiling Captain Jolly Roger sold his old fishing tug and purchased a nice little boat to haul people back and forth. Roger was a half Jamaican, half Irish gent who had developed into one of my best friends on di island, which was saying a lot given my warm and fuzzy feelings towards most everyone around me. I was glad he was doing well with his little enterprise, but it didn't help Gus make a living.

"Do you know if Gus brought that replacement valve for the fermenter with him?" I asked.

"I'm not sure," said Boyd. "He did have some packages and letters. Oh, and maybe you'll want to grab one of Rodrigo's discount coupons before they're all gone."

"Discount coupons?" I said.

"Yeah, Rodrigo sent Wonbago a stack of ten percent off coupons to hand out for a stay at he and his brother's Best Western in Boise," said Boyd.

"Ugh; no thank you," I said. "Anything else interesting arrive with him?"

"Just a woman," said Boyd. "Attractive, actually. A blonde, decked out in Banana Republic type gear."

"Maybe Brittany hunted me down; she probably wants the crock pot now that she's had time to think about it, but she'll have to talk to Marty's wife on that one," I said.

"I doubt this woman is her; from what I could overhear of she and Gus' conversation, this gal seemed nice," said Boyd. "Maybe you two can hook up later; it will be couple's night at the Monkey, after all."

Ever since Isabella had gone corporate on me, it seemed like everyone on di island had been trying to set me up. But other than the daily turistas that passed quickly through, it was a small island with limited female choices, most of whom were well established as my friends. "Couple's night? When did that start?" I asked.

"Today is the first. You order one Red Stripe, and you get a couple. One Pickled Parrot, and you get a couple," said Boyd. "Etc, etc. And whether you want two or not."

"So why doesn't the Innkeeper just call it two for one, then?" I said.

"He told me he thought couple's night sounded more romantic; I think he's still trying to get back the customers he lost to Henri," said Boyd.

"At least it's a bargain for a change," I said.

"Not really; you order one and you get a couple; and you pay for a couple. You know the Innkeeper," said Boyd.

I scowled. "Yeah, he's the most interesting *and* cheapest innkeeper in the world," I said.

"Ain't that the truth," said Boyd.

We chatted for a while longer, both of us forestalling what passed for our work. Eventually we said our goodbyes and he headed back to swim in Mother Ocean, and I got cleaned up, then pointed my compass towards Father Rum.

I would have liked to hang out in my little corner of di island for a while longer before heading towards civilization. Maybe have a swim, or take a nap now that I was awake and could. But something was pulling me away. I couldn't put my finger on what it was, just that something was different today. I'd grown accustomed to all the little nuances of di island. And whenever something somewhat out of the ordinary was about to happen, I could feel it on the breeze, like a coming change in the climate. And right now my inner barometer was on the move, so I felt the need to be too, like a crazy storm chaser.

It looked like the weather was here; I hoped it'd be beautiful.

Chapter 3
"A rum pirate looks at 80."

I walked through the newly built employee door at the back of the building, and onto the floor of Di Island Rum Company factory. We'd had to install the new entrance once tours became a fairly regular occurrence, leaving the big front doors locked to keep the nosy, shutter snapping, foreign raiders from invading rum land unescorted. It was either that or keep Jedidiah posted out front to scare them away, a tomato sauce stained machete in his big hand.

I was stopping by for my daily what's up with di rum check-in. It was hardly necessary anymore, which might explain why it was hardly daily anymore either, but it made me feel almost like a productive member of society to go through the motions. Looking around, I wondered if there hadn't been some sort of mutiny, or more closely, that everyone hadn't abandoned ship; nobody was around, only Bob singing the Redemption Song over the sound system. Then I realized that like always, I'd timed my arrival during the lunch hour. So I made my way past the pot stills and out onto the patio overlooking the ocean, where I found my lost staff, seated and standing amidst the umbrella covered tables.

"Boss! Come and sit over here!" yelled Faith.

I went over to her table, exchanging greetings with people as I went, and sat down next to she and Cavin. "Good morning," I said.

"It's afternoon, not morning," said Cavin, a bit grumpily.

"I know; that's what's so good about it," I said. I may not have minded getting out of bed now, but that didn't mean I was in a close, loving relationship with mornings; my reconciliation with the AM had only gone so far.

"Some of us have been awake and working for a long time already," said Faith.

"Do I detect a little chastisement in there?" I said, helping myself to a jerk chicken leg from the plate on the table.

"No, you're di boss," said Faith. "If you want to sleep in, you should sleep in."

"Thanks," I said.

"It's just sometimes I miss when we weren't quite so busy," said Faith.

It was true; our rum was selling well. While we weren't exactly knocking Batman Ron and Cap'n Henry Morgan off the shelves, orders were coming in quickly enough to put a strain on our tiny little factory's output capacity. Luis really wanted us to expand, but I was firmly against it. I wasn't trying to get rich, and I didn't want to ruin the quaintness and persona of our little company. And if that meant we sometimes fell behind in our shipments, so be it; we were Di Island Rum Company, and we promised to put a little of our islanditude into every bottle. I wanted to live up to that promise, even if it meant those bottles were occasionally tardy.

"I know what you mean; there's always a lot of work to do around here now, isn't there? I'm lucky to have you, Luis, and Cavin here to run the day to day things so I can continue my dual career as a beach bum and slackaholic," I said, then looked around. "Where is Luis, anyway?"

"He didn't come in to work again today," said Cavin.

"Is he alright?" I said.

Faith shrugged. "He's been under di weather all week," she said. "I'm beginning to worry about him, boss."

I was, too. Although he always seemed happy enough (when he wasn't grumbling at me over my continued lack of rum knowledge), Luis hadn't been himself for some time now, often going home early or missing work altogether. And when he was at the factory he moved slower, like he was tired.

I didn't mind from an owner's point of view; the factory kept on going when he wasn't around, thanks in part to all he had done to get us started, and if he needed to rest it was fine by me. And Cavin had shown great aptitude for the rum business, being smart, hard working, and artistic, so our future looked as sunny as the present. But I worried about Luis, my very good friend.

"I'll stop by his place and see how he's doing," I said.

"Say hi for me," said Faith. "And tell him we miss him; Cavin is a slave driver when he's not here."

"I just think we should do things a certain way," said Cavin.

"So do I; *our* way," said Faith.

"Your way is too old fashioned and slow," said Cavin.

"And that's why di rum comes out tasting so good," said Faith. "It feels relaxed."

Cavin scowled. "That's a great big load of bull-"

"Well, I can see you two have a lot to talk about," I said, standing up. "Is there anything I should know before I go someplace else so you two can argue properly?"

"No, di rum is fine," said Faith.

"Just a little behind the times," said Cavin, and Faith stuck her tongue out at him.

"Oh, Ernesto wanted me to ask if you could come to di sugar plantation today," said Faith.

I sighed. I didn't do much around here, but most of it seemed to consist of walking back and forth from the plantation, and I do mean walking. My old Indian motorcycle was in time out mode ever since it and an iguana I tried to avoid had decided to team up to throw me, giving me a nasty case of dirt road rash and a renewed sense of self preservation. "What's wrong now?" I asked.

"He just wanted your advice on-" began Faith.

"-something sugar cane related?" I finished.

"Yes," said Faith.

"Look; tell him this. I love your hubby, and I'm very happy having him run the plantation, but *he's* the sugar expert, not me. That's why I hired him, to make all the decisions. Because I couldn't keep a plastic cactus alive, let alone an entire field of sugar cane," I said. "So from now on, when he finds something where he's not sure what to do, I want him to remind himself that I'd have *no idea* what to do, other than something stupid that would end up killing all the plants, and that he's gonna have to figure it out for himself. Got it?"

"Got it, boss," said Faith. "I'll tell him to stop pestering you so much."

"Thanks," I said.

"And I'll tell him you love him," said Faith, smiling.

"You do that," I said. "Just don't getting jealous on us."

And my work was done for another day.

I usually didn't see the point of hanging around the factory getting in everyone's way, though I did like to be there whenever another batch of rum was born, so it would know who its father was. Other than that, I popped my head in, checked the factory for fires and the patio for cute tourists, maybe grabbing a bite or a drink from the patio bar and grill, and then took myself elsewhere. Today nothing was burning and the tourists hadn't arrived yet, which meant it was time for me to be useless some place more useful.

So like Elvis I left the building and headed east down the familiar dirt road, thinking as I went about how much Cavin had grown up over the last year. He was like a different person, taking his responsibilities at the factory very seriously. It was great to see, and at the same time, a little sad. It's hard to take on new aspects to our personalities without losing others, and some of his youthful exuberance was gone. But then again, maybe it had just gone into hiding for a while, waiting to reemerge somewhere down the road when it was needed most. Such as after too damned much of that seriousness.

My thoughts were interrupted when a small herd of loudly chattering German tourists approached and passed me, the men in socks and sandals, the women looking a little flushed from walking in the hot sun. It was a particularly warm day today, and one thing di island hadn't developed yet was any sort of taxi service. I guessed they were probably on the way to the factory, which was a good, healthy stroll for anyone from the docks, even robust, young, German fraüleins.

I wasn't sure yet how I felt about having all these new visitors to di island every day. So far they hadn't created any serious problems, and for the most part it was a lot of fun meeting people from every corner of the globe. But there had been a few nights when Monkey Drool's had gotten pretty rowdy, and not necessarily in a good way. So suddenly Jedidiah was moonlighting as a peace officer, something we had never needed before. No one was quite sure what we were going to do if he had to arrest somebody since we didn't have a jail, but luckily it hadn't come to that yet. A six foot six, angry looking man with shoulders and arms like a Banyan tree was all the crime deterrent we'd needed so far.

When I came to the old wooden mailbox by the side of the road, I turned south down the path towards Luis' cottage. I found him seated outside in his flower garden, under the shade of a big thatched umbrella. He looked to be asleep, his head bowed, and I quietly sat down in the chair across from him.

I watched him for a few long moments; he was very still, and I tried to decide if he was breathing or not. I felt like I should check, but I was afraid of what I might find; it seemed better to just let him sleep, even if that wasn't what he was doing.

"I am not dead yet, so you can stop worrying about it, Jack," he said suddenly.

I sighed a sigh of relief. "I didn't think you were, Luis," I said.

"Yes, you did. Everyone thinks I am about to go rush off for a visit to Heaven; especially Faith," said Luis, sitting up slowly.

"I'm not sure you could just visit; that Saint Pete's kind of a one way doorman," I said. "How did you know it was me, anyway?"

"I could see your feet; you are the only one on di island who wears Margaritaville flip-flops," said Luis. "Except for some of those tourists out of Key West, and they better stay out of my garden if they know what is good for them. I suppose you are here to see how I am doing?"

"No, I just thought I'd stop in for a visit," I said.

"You are worse at lying than you are at tasting rum," said Luis, then he thought about it. "Never mind; no one is that bad at lying."

"Well, I'm good at drinking di rum, and that's all I care about," I said. I leaned back in my chair, more relaxed now that I found Luis to be his feisty, crabby, and very much alive self. "So if you already know why I'm here, Luis, you can tell me how you're feeling."

"Lousy," said Luis.

"What seems to be the problem?" I said, in my best doctorese.

"I am old," said Luis.

"I'm afraid I can't help you there," I said. "Part of the price we pay for living very long."

"Not a very good reward for putting up with people's bullshit for this many years," said Luis, then he looked around him. "Still, I suppose I am happy; it has been a good life."

"You probably shouldn't talk about your life in the past tense," I said. "You don't want it to get the wrong impression."

"Yes, but Jack, when you reach your very last moment, everything *is* past tense," said Luis, shaking his head.

I looked at him closely; it was hard to judge him sometimes. He was a complicated person, able to make use of as many conflicting emotions in any given situation as he could flavors in a bottle of rum. "Are you saying you're unhappy?" I tentatively asked. "Because I thought you just said you were-"

"No, I am not saying that!" he said, almost in the same tone of voice he used when I couldn't tell vanilla from caramel. "Just the opposite. I have been sitting here thinking and wondering how I would be feeling if you had never come along and opened the rum factory, and I had never gotten the chance to make my own rum."

"Oh, that," I said, then shrugged modestly. "I just did what I did like I always do; you give me too much credit."

"I know; I do," said Luis.

I blinked at him. "You do?"

"Yes. Don't get me wrong," he said, leaning forward and putting a hand on my knee. "I am very grateful that you did what you did. But if I had never made my rum, would my life have been so worthless? I think not. I have many good friends, like you, and many good memories. That is far more important than what I might or might not have accomplished."

"Er, good," I said, a little confused all of a sudden about my place in things. "I'm glad you feel that way."

"I wanted you to know that more than anyone else, Jack," said Luis. "Because for someone who says he does not think about the past or the future, you still worry too much. Just be happy, because in the end that is all you will have. And happy is what I am, so when I go, I want you to be glad for me."

I was even more confused now, since I could have sworn happy was what I was, too, sometimes ridiculously so. But I wasn't about to argue with him; I'd just lose like always, since he was a lot smarter and wiser than I was.

Instead I stood up, and went over and put my hand on his shoulder. "Alright, my friend; I promise," I said. "*When* you go, twenty or thirty years from now, I'll do a little dance for you."

"You had better; I will be watching you, Jack," said Luis.

"Good; Uncle Billy and I can always use another quality ghost in the family," I said.

As I left Luis' little plot of heaven, I decided he seemed to be okay. He was probably just a little tired; I knew I planned to be when I reached his age. I was already welcoming more and more naps into my life, and I hadn't even reached the age we pirates were supposed to start looking at yet. At the rate I was going I was liable to be comatose by the time I was forty years past it like Luis was, and I figured he'd more than earned his right to take time off to relax whenever he felt the need.

I made my way back to Rum Boulevard, the street that ran west to east across di island; you could tell things were changing when our four main dirt roads suddenly needed to have names. From there, my flip-flops soon carried me into the Crossroads area, which too, was rapidly changing. Besides the new farm and hardware supply store the Clarkes of Barbados had opened, there was also now a clothing store, a grocery store, and of all things, a sporting goods store.

I thought Pat from Canada had been a little overly optimistic opening the latter, since most of di islanders preferred a leisurely stroll or swim in the ocean for their daily dose of exercise to the high-tech treadmill he stubbornly displayed in his front window. But Pat had a dream, and that dream was to get as far away from snow blowers, twenty degrees, and hockey games as he could, and I definitely rooted for him to succeed. I just wasn't sure selling soccer balls and skateboards to the younger crowd would be enough to keep him from going out of business. Then again, Mr. Wonbago had purchased a set of golf clubs from him, and now spent the day putting around his office in his new green suit jacket, waiting for the Masters to wise up and move from Augusta National to di island. I guess you never know where potential customers might come from, so maybe Pat had a chance to hold on to his piece of paradise after all.

I popped into the market and bought a basket of island strawberries to munch on, then continued east down Coconut Lane. I was in a particularly good mood, bursting with a kind of unfamiliar energy. It seemed like almost too much happy for one person, and I suddenly felt a sharp desire to share it with someone else. So naturally I told my flip-flops to take me straight to Monkey Drool's.

Not that I would have had to say anything; I could have just wandered around aimlessly for a while, letting them drive, and sooner or later we probably would have gotten there anyway. It seemed they were often of the opinion the Monkey was where I needed to be, and I saw little reason to question their wisdom. One should never argue with open-toed footwear.

But today I was in a hurry for some reason, and requested a more direct route. I wasn't sure what the hell was driving me at first, but when I got to Monkey Drool's and went out back and looked around, I suddenly knew what my *unfamiliar energy* was all about. I'd been without female companionship ever since Isabella's departure, which had been fine by me up until now. But when I saw *her* sitting at the bar, and felt my libido rip off its black funeral dress shirt, sending buttons flying, only to pull on its multicolored, tie-dyed, *"let's party!"* tee instead, I knew my sex drive had finally and robustly emerged from its period of mourning.

To put it in more scientific terms, Jack was suddenly horny.

Chapter 4
"Who's di blonde stranger?"

My first impression of the woman was that she was attractive.

My second impression was the same, just with a *very* added to it.

She had shortish blonde hair, lightly tousled in the salt air breeze that was blowing in from the nearby ocean. I'd never really been a fan of shorter hair on a woman, at least until that moment; anyone and everyone I'd ever been infatuated with in the past had had a long, flowing mane. But it suited her perfectly, and suddenly my tastes seemed to change as quickly as they had with my first sip of real island rum.

I assumed she was the gal who'd arrived with Gus this morning that Boyd had mentioned. She was sitting at Monkey Drool's, next of course to the Coconut Motel he said she'd been headed to. And she was dressed in a white cargo shirt and olive cargo shorts, that looked like they'd probably come straight from a Banana Republic or Tommy Bahama cargo crate. Circumstantial evidence at its best I know, but *if* it was her, it meant she'd be staying at least one night at the motel. And right now I desperately wanted her to be staying for at least one night.

I gave my best shot at nonchalantly sidling towards she and the bar, even though nonchalantly wasn't one of my stronger adverbs, and I'd never much had the knack for it. The overall effect was probably that of a crab stalking a dead fish, and many fathoms below my mentor George Clooney's sex appeal range. Thankfully I lucked out and she didn't look up, and didn't seem to notice my crustacean like approach.

The Innkeeper, however, did.

"Mister Jack!" he said exuberantly, with a big smile and a wave. "Come in, come in!"

The woman turned her head slightly to look at me with a casual glance, then locked her brown eyes on mine, which was very disconcerting; we sneaking crabs don't function well under the direct gaze of our prey, who are supposed to wait unaware for us to come over and begin to nibble on them.

"Are you hurt, Mister Jack?" said the Innkeeper, something he'd started calling me a few months ago. "You look like you be limpin'."

"I stepped on a pop-top," I said, trying to be funny in a clinch. The woman managed a little smirk, or more likely, charitably allowed me one. I finished my long skitter to the bar and sat down next to her.

"What can I get for you, Mister Jack?" said the Innkeeper.

I thought about it. "Do you have any Toucans back there?" I asked, looking for some quick liquid fortification.

"Coming right up," the Innkeeper said. He puttered around for a few long seconds getting my drink, while I nervously waited for something to nervously sip on, then plopped two coconut mugs in front of me. Obviously the new Couple's Night started early at the Monkey, since I already had a small phlock to protect me. And two toucans would definitely do it better than one toucan can.

"I've got those," said the woman.

"Thanks," I said, hoping the rest of our relationship would be as sunny as this early weather report was indicating.

"No problem; you're just the man I've been wanting to see," she said, turning on her barstool to face me.

I wondered if there was a weather term for sunnier than sunny. "I am?" I said, picking up my drink and taking a long pull on the straw.

"Yep," she said, grabbing her own coco cup and clunking mine, causing me to take a second long drink. Then she looked at me from under her long lashes. "You're Jack Danielson, right?"

I had to stop and think for a moment, but then confidently said, "Yes; yes, I am."

"I'm Kaitlyn Mars," she said, putting out her hand. I took it and shook it, and she added, "Everyone tells me you're the big kahuna around here."

"They're exaggerating," I said, although I had to admit I liked the sound of this new title she'd bestowed me with.

"So you don't own Di Island Rum Company?" asked Kaitlyn.

"No, I do," I said.

"And the Sugar Daddy Plantation?" said Kaitlyn. She had a slight drawl, like a southerner who'd spent some time away from her kind, perhaps in the east.

"I do own that too, yes; although the name is still up for debate," I said.

"That's about two-thirds of the economy around here, isn't it?" she asked.

"Closer to tree-fourths," the Innkeeper piped in helpfully. I gave him my *"go away I'm talking to a girl"* look, but he ignored it like di islanders did all my looks.

"I don't know; di island is growing pretty quickly these days," I said. "It's getting harder to tell where all the dineros are flowing to and from."

"Thanks to you," said Kaitlyn.

"Maybe," I said. "Does that have something to do with why you were looking for me?"

"In a way," she said. "I need someone to show me di island and figured you'd be the perfect guide, since everyone seems to respect you and you own so much of it."

Now the day was being just plain silly, and I could hear Mr. Rogers singing in my ear about how beautiful things were in the neighborhood. "I'd be glad to, but I still don't see why you want me," I said, always looking gift sea ponies in the mouth. "Other than being the one to luck into the rum factory and plantation, why am I so qualified? What do you do, anyway?"

"I'm in tourism," said Kaitlyn. "I work for a company that checks places out to see what they're like."

"That sounds a little vague," I said.

"That's because it *is* a little vague," said Kaitlyn. "But it's what I do for a living."

I decided I wasn't exactly in any position to question her career, considering my past experience in public relations hammering the dings out of company's images, another vague job. "Then I'm your man," I said, hoping that might turn out to be totally true, in some sweaty, sticky manner. "What do you want to see first?"

Kaitlyn looked around. "The ocean looks like a good start. Why don't we take our drinks to that table so we can chat?" she said, pointing to a spot down by the beach.

We picked up our coconuts and made our way to the table and sat down, leaving the Innkeeper behind to practice his lip reading.

"So what would you like to talk about?" I said.

"Well, everyone's already told me all about you, and how you came to be here, the rum factory, and all that," said Kaitlyn. "So why don't you just tell me about di island?"

"That's a pretty broad subject," I said.

"Then just describe it like you were going to Tweet about it to someone who's never been here; what would you type?" said Kaitlyn.

"How many letters do I get again? Something like nine?" I said.

"A hundred and forty, actually," said Kaitlyn. "I counted once."

"All I know is that it's always about three too few," I said.

"Give it a shot," said Kaitlyn. "You can fudge a little, but not too much; we don't want to anger the Bluebird of Twitter Happiness."

I thought about how to sum up my haven and what it meant to me in one tiny package. It may have been small, but di island still didn't want to fit inside the box. I found my best hope was little words or phrases, like a bunch of short Tweets, that put together might get some small fraction of my thoughts and feelings across.

"Paradise. Home. Friends. Simple. No worries. Unspoiled. Enjoyment. No bullshit," I said. I did a quick calculation and found I still had quite a few characters left after all. "Life as it should always be."

"So what you're trying to tell me is you sort of like it here," Kaitlyn said wryly.

"You could say that," I said.

"Can you say why, more specifically?" she said. "I mean, besides the weather, and beaches, and palm trees; that's the obvious stuff."

"It's hard to put into words," I said. "It's the same way I felt when I was in the French Quarter and Key West. It's a sense of contentedness, like I finally don't have a reason to be someplace else. Time slows down, and so do your heart rate and your mind. You just are who you are and where you are."

Kaitlyn sat watching me speak, and I watched her watch me back. I realized I hadn't exactly been that much more specific. And that she had light freckles across her nose.

"And di islanders are great people. They're friendly, warm, and a unique bunch. You can walk pretty much anywhere you want to get to, and we have three good places to eat. And rum; lots of rum," I said.

"I can't imagine why someone wouldn't enjoy visiting here. If they didn't, it would be their fault, not di island's. Or di islander's. Or the rum's."

"So five stars then, eh?" said Kaitlyn.

"At least," I said. "But without the concierge and the limo service to your beach villa. If you're looking for that, you're shit out of luck here."

Kaitlyn sat quietly for a moment, then said, "It sounds nice. I'm looking forward to really getting to know the place."

"So you're staying here for a while then?" I said hopefully, sounding like a kid who just found out from his parents that he might be going to Disney World. I wondered if I'd get the chance to spend any time in Fantasyland...

"For a week or two, for sure," said Kaitlyn. "Maybe longer. It depends."

Maybe even enough time for my methodical and cowardly moves to take down any defenses she might have, brick by brick. "Then do you want to go check out some of di island right now?" I said.

Kaitlyn looked around, smiled, then shrugged. "Not really. I'm sitting near the ocean, sipping on something fruity and delicious, while my toes wriggle in the sand. Like you said before, I don't see any good reason to move at the moment."

"So your job right now is to check out this spot?" I said.

"That's what they pay me for," she said, raising her coconut mug.

It sounded like a tough gig, and I wondered why my high school counselor hadn't pointed out any sit on the beach and drink career opportunities to *me* way back when; it would have saved me a lot of stress on my long spiritual journey to di island. Then again, my aptitude tests had likely shown I wasn't particularly qualified at the time. But I was more than up to the task now.

And for the rest of the afternoon I proved it.

A few hours later, just as the sun was melting into the water on the other side of di island, I found myself lying in the hammock the Innkeeper had hung from two of the palm trees between Monkey Drool's and the Coconut Motel. Jolly Roger had told him about the ones peppering the area around the Soggy dollar in Tortola, and how nice it was to have a place to recline into a truly laid back position. So the Innkeeper, always in competition with that *other* beach bar he'd heard about but never seen, had simply had to keep up with the Virgin Island Joneses once again by adding a couple of hammocks of his own. It was always uphill work against a great place like the Soggy Dollar, but I loved my Monkey dearly and wouldn't have traded it for any amount of moistened money.

I wouldn't have switched over to any of their hammocks at the moment, either. Because although I'd be hard pressed to explain exactly how or why the hell it had happened, I wasn't alone in my knotted net, and was squeezed up against Kaitlyn in that pleasing way that only a hammock can provide. It turned out she fit inside and under my arm in a most delightful manner, as if she had been tailor fit for just such a purpose.

Gazing at Kaitlyn lying there snuggled up against me made me wonder if I was in someplace special, where two songs become one (and I'm not talking about the horizontal mambo). We'd just harmonized instantly, as if we'd been jamming together for years, but unlike some bands (such as Brittany and I) were still playing in tune. And other than thinking about it right now, for once I'd just sat back and let the music play.

And maybe that's why things had gone like they had this time, since I've usually had a tendency to try too hard when mating rituals began. If I'd been a parrot, for instance, I would have scared off most of my potential phemale phriends with all my tail and wing flapping, strutting, and nervous squawking about. But with Kaitlyn I'd been one cool, laid back bird. It would be great to discover it meant that sometimes the best moves were no moves at all, since I didn't have any to begin with, but I suspected I'd just gotten lucky this time, even if I hadn't as of yet (gotten lucky, that is).

Our feet were intertwined on the upper end of the hammock, covered in sand from our wade in the ocean followed by our barefoot walk to our current locale. If we human's lower paws ever truly manage any aesthetic value, it's probably while they're blanketed in those tiny little rocks; it beats the hell out of having them coated with any wool, rayon, or cotton fibers, along with the ever accompanying sweat, that's for sure. The sand just feels good, and having your feet covered in it is a reminder you've been strolling someplace special.

I could tell my hammock companion was napping, which didn't sound like such a bad idea. It had been a long afternoon of things to make one feel content and drowsy; from our conversation surrounded by sand, surf, and sun, to the cornucopia of fruit flavors we'd sampled while making our was through the Innkeeper's ever expanding drink menu, to the spicy jambalaya we'd had on the deck down at Robichaux's. And nodding off to a short sleep session seemed the perfect desert to accompany those previous hours.

I let my eyes close and listened to Kaitlyn softly breathing, barely audible over the rustling of the palm trees above, and the splashing of the nearby ocean. I would have been happy to stay in that state of borderline consciousness for hours, if not days, but there wasn't an insomniac on Earth that wouldn't have fallen asleep under those conditions, and I was no exception.

I didn't dream, maybe because it would have been a bit mundane after the waking day I'd already experienced. I just slept, slowly recharging my 12 volt battery for the grand finale, when I woke to Kaitlyn's lips an hour or so later.

And the rest of the night is none of your damned business.

Chapter 5
"That's how I came to meet my American friend."

People I know from my dark ages on the mainland tell me time and time again through letters and phone calls (the latter during the sporadic times my cell phone hasn't gone swimming in Mother Ocean) that they're convinced my recreational hours all involve drinking. That isn't true at all; I spend a great many days stone cold sober, and am fully able to enjoy those times with the best of those folks who like to waggle a finger at anyone who chooses to imbibe. But I will let you in on my dirty little secret; I *do* like to drink. If I didn't, and still drank, *then* I'd be worried about myself.

I'm not saying I love to get wasted, blackout, and generally turn into a stumbling slur machine. I'd prefer that never happened, but I am a human, which means I over indulge in whatever I happen to be doing from time to time. What I enjoy though is how it tends to make people more social. If we were all as friendly as we are after a few cocktails we'd be a lot better off, maybe because once our minds get a little fuzzy we forget just how bad we think the world is, and how everybody in it but us is to blame. Drinking is one of the few things that helps bring folks together, so in that way it's like a religion, except you don't see the wine drinkers killing the beer drinkers over who's way of drinking is the one true way.

I'm not even sure why I bring it up, other than the fact that as a single male without a family, so many of my fondest memories *do* seem to involve alcohol in some way, something that worried me for a short time. I met Brittany at a party (and yes, that is a fond memory again, now) and Isabella at Monkey Drool's. My whole vacation of self awareness was peppered with boat drinks and beers, and I've lost track of the number of beach gatherings and rum rumbles I've attended since moving to di island, all memorable. And what I've found is this; even when you add me to the six thousand plus years that people have been partying up a storm, the world and civilization as we know it haven't come to an end, something that probably would have happened a long time ago if we hadn't found a way to unwind. And at the very least, most of us wouldn't even have been born without the aid of our liquid Cupid bartender somewhere back in our ancestry. So I'm going to keep doing what I do and enjoy it.

I'd like to think though that fermentation wasn't the reason I woke up the next morning in one of the Innkeeper's rooms at the Coconut Motel. Kaitlyn wasn't by my side, but that was only because she'd sneaked out on me some time after the sun had come up. Under normal conditions it would have been the perfect situation; no awkward moments trying to figure out how the other person felt about having mated with you during the night, and even more importantly, no worrying about your breath. But I felt quite good about the night before, and had absolutely no regrets, and wished Kaitlyn was still there to wake up to and make me smile some more. But that wasn't the case, so I got up, did what I could to make myself presentable, and walked over to Monkey Drool's to see if she might be there.

She wasn't, so I went home and further polished myself up, then went out to search di island. I didn't know if Kaitlyn wanted me to look for her or not, but I did know *I* wanted to find *her*. I'd thoroughly enjoyed our day together, including the stretch leading up to the flopping about like seals part, and I looked forward to her company while showing her around di island.

I had no idea where she was likely to be, and since I was hungry and the Cantina was the nearest spot for me to eat, I thought it would be as good a place as any to check first and cross off my list. But as it turned out, halfway through my curried pork with plantain hash, I was the one who got found.

"There you are! Do you have any idea how hard you are to get a hold of?"

I turned to look, and wasn't at all surprised to find that it wasn't Kaitlyn, since the voice had been a little on the masculine side. I was however, surprised by who it did turn out to be.

"Marty!" I said, leaping clumsily out of my chair. We did the manly hug thing, then sat down at my table. "What the hell are you doing here?"

"Do I need a reason to visit my friend?" said Marty.

"I'm assuming yes, and that you finally came up with one, since I've been trying in vain to get you to come down here for two years now," I said.

"Goes to show what you know," said Marty. "A couple of nights ago I was back in Minnesota, sitting in Andy's Saloon. Another blizzard was hitting the area, and I could see through the window that the snow was really beginning to pile up outside. The weather girl on TV, you know, the evil one, was smiling another one of her cheesy grins while she ruthlessly announced that even more of Old Man Winter's dandruff was gonna be coming the next day. I thought about my driveway and my broken down snow blower, and then I thought of you, sitting down here in the sun. And how the closest you probably come to having a shovel in your hand is when you carry your little plastic bucket and pail down to the beach to build sandcastles."

"I don't build sandcastles; it's too much work, and I suck at sculpting," I said.

"Just illustrates my point all the more," said Marty. "And that point is, I wondered to myself what the hell I was doing *there*, went to the airport, jumped on a plane, and arrived at di island so you could ask me what the hell I was doing *here*."

"Well, when did you get *here?*" I asked.

"About an hour ago; I took Jolly Roger's shuttle over from Tortola," said Marty.

I looked around. "Then where's your luggage?" I asked.

"Don't have any; like I said, I jumped on a plane," said Marty. "Unless you want to count this tote bag I bought at the market across the way. See?" and he held up a tan burlap bag, with the official *"I love di island!"* logo printed upon it. "I thought I should have something to put all the stuff I buy in."

"You mean, like that tee shirt you're wearing?" I said, pointing.

Marty proudly puffed out his chest, which didn't make a lot of difference, since he'd spent most of his life in a cubicle. But it did show off his Fish Gutter tee, which depicted a school of fish fleeing in terror from a machete wielding madman (not an easy thing to depict). Da Fish Gutter building down by the docks had been converted into a gift shop with the same name, selling seashells by the sea shore, as well as shirts and hats with Jedidiah's crazy designs on them. The place was a big hit with the tourists, and evidently, with Marty. "I'm just going to buy what I need as I go," he said.

"And you needed that shirt," I said.

"Actually, I did," said Marty, sullenly. "The ocean was a little rough today, and so was last night at the Soggy Dollar Bar. Those Painkillers you told me about are smooth going down, but not so smooth coming back up, and they don't look good on a maroon polo."

"Ugh. I see," I said. "Are you hungry at all, then?"

"Yeah, I think I'm recovered enough to eat; what you're having looks good," said Marty.

I motioned to Terrance and ordered another plate of hash, today's Cantina lunch special, and a few minutes later Marty and I continued our conversation.

"So you just dropped everything and came to visit," I said. "How did your wife feel about that?"

"Bonnie?" asked Marty.

"Yeah, that one," I said.

Marty stirred his hash around and stared down at it. "We're not doing so good, actually," he said. "In fact, I think it's over."

"What?!" I said. "When did that happen?"

"It finished right about now, but I think it started when she made me quit working for you," said Marty. "Remember?"

I sighed. "Yes, I do; she said you were gone too much, and the benefits I gave you weren't good enough with two kids. She might have been right about that last part, but it was all I could afford while we were getting started."

"I understood," said Marty. "But I was happy for a change. And Bonnie making me get my job back at Image Makers, that was tough to swallow. I should have burned my bridges with them like you did."

This was all a bit of a shock to me; I'd known Marty wasn't always a happy camper, but talking about the end of a nine year marriage, with kids, that was something I hadn't expected. And certainly not over curried pork at the Cantina on di island. "So what are you gonna do now?" I said.

"I just did it," said Marty. "I'm here now."

"What do you mean?" I said.

"On di island. I'm done with everything back home; this is where I live and work now, if you have a job for me," said Marty. "But I'm not going back. Bonnie can have the house, the cars, everything. And Strickland at Image Makers can kiss my ass so long. This time, for good."

I began to understand how insane it must have seemed when I'd broken up with Brittany, quit my own job, sold everything I owned, and hit the road. But I'd been single, or at least, just had a girlfriend, and one that didn't like me very much. This seemed vastly different. But then again, if it was what Marty had to do to be happy...

I decided to just let it be for now. Even if I wanted to try and talk my friend out of what he was doing to his life, now probably wasn't the time. I figured I'd give Marty a few days to realize the true consequences of his actions, which would also give me a few days to ponder over which side of the fence to be on. And if I even wanted to get involved; sometimes it's best to have a non-interference policy, like the Star Trek Federation's prime directive.

"Of course I'd have a job for you. You did great getting the rum promoted when we were starting up," I said. "But not right now; why don't you spend a week or two just hanging around relaxing. After we're done eating I'll get you set up at my house at the plantation; you can stay there, and you'll have everything you need. Just watch out for Ernesto; he's liable to ask you for advice on the sugar cane."

"Thanks," said Marty. "I could use some down time."

"Can't we all?" I said.

Eventually I took my old friend up to the big house, and then down to Monkey Drool's. If he wanted to relax, the Monkey was always willing to help, and I thought perhaps Kaitlyn would be back at the motel. She wasn't, but we ran into Cavin, who said she'd been at the rum factory a short time ago and had headed down to the nearby beach. So I had a quick cocktail with Marty, introduced him to a couple of di islanders, and trucked back towards my place yet again.

It was turning into just the sort of hiking day that kept me out of Pat's sporting good shop, and kept the body that carted my consciousness around slender no matter how many boat drinks I fed it. I'd already gone from the eastern side of di island to the western side, then into the center, up to the north, back to the east, and now had to truck all the way to the western shore again. That basically meant I'd crossed di island four times now, so I was pretty happy that island wasn't Greenland. I was however, thinking it was about time to let my motorcycle out of time out mode.

And that one of these days I need to figure out why relaxing on an island keeps turning out to be so strenuous.

Chapter 6
"I have found her at home."

I finally found Kaitlyn, and in of all places, standing in my front yard. And just like when I'd run into Marty, and nine out of ten people who spend hours looking for me with no results, I got the usual response from her; right after the unusual kiss she gave me, that is.

"There you are! Do you have any idea how hard you are to get a hold of?" she said.

"Yes, as a matter of fact, I do," I said. "But I like it that way. And I have been looking for you, too, you know, so evidently you're just as hard to reach."

Kaitlyn pulled a cell out of her cutoff jeans and waggled it at me. "This is a portable phone; we humans invented them a few years back," she said, with a wry smile.

"...and we invented shoes even farther back, but I don't have much use for those anymore, either," I said. "Although I have to admit, cell phones do make great paperweights, once you quiet them down with a little sea water."

Kaitlyn put her phone away, and pointed the 35mm camera that hung around her neck at my hut and took a picture. "Do you know who lives here?" she asked.

"Yes, as another matter of fact, I know that too," I said. "It's me."

Kaitlyn turned and looked at me in surprise. "You do?" she said. "But I thought you lived on the plantation."

"No, my friend Marty, from Minnesota, lives there," I said.

"There's two of you from Minnesota here on di island?" she asked.

"As of today, yeah," I said. Kaitlyn continued to stare at me, as if she were waiting for a more thorough explanation. "It's a long story, filled with all sorts of things I don't want to talk about right now. How about I give you the grand tour of my home instead?"

"Okay," she said, and we walked up and into my thatched palace. I carefully pointed out the highlights (fridge, bed, boombox, frozen concoction maker), which took all of about three minutes, then we went back out and had a seat on the porch.

We sat there quietly for a few moments, then Kaitlyn said, "It's simple."

"That's why I like it," I said. "You don't?"

"No, it's not that; it just isn't where I'd expect the wealthiest person on di island to live," she said.

"Sometimes the best part of being wealthy is doing what you want, or living where you want," I said. "And I'd hardly call myself wealthy. Not money wise, anyway; maybe in other things."

Kaitlyn looked around at my natural beach habitat. "It is nice here, I've got to admit; how are the sunsets?"

"Oh, they range from stunning to exquisite to spectacular to extraordinary," I said. "Then there are the really good ones."

"Sounds like a perfect spot," said Kaitlyn.

"The best on di island," I said, proudly. "Of course, I still need to prove it by showing you the rest of the place."

"Um, I'm pretty sure I've seen most everything already. I went to have breakfast at Robichaux's while you were sleeping, and ran into a guy named Crazy Chester, and he took me on a tour," said Kaitlyn. "Sorry, I tried to wake you."

"Chester's here, too? What is this, reunion week?" I said. The Chetster had been awol for some time now, ever since Akiko had sold the market to Terrance and Geeah, and moved to the Keys to help run Crazy Chester's Bar and Boat Stop. There still hadn't been any wedding buoy bells ringing out across the ocean, and there were no immediate plans to make things between the two of them *official*. But then Chester wasn't one to truck much with official anyway; he still did battle with any establishments who had a problem with his no shoes and no shirt forever philosophy, and said they should be damned glad he bothered with pants. I couldn't agree with him more; I know *I* was glad he bothered.

"Are you disappointed your friend beat you to it?" asked Kaitlyn.

"Yes," I said, poutily. "I was looking forward to it."

"Well, you could show me the big docks up north; that was the one thing we skipped. Chester said they were in enemy territory; something about a blood feud between he and a dead pirate?" said Kaitlyn. "I didn't ask."

"Hm; I wonder what that's all about," I said. "I haven't heard anything about an argument between those two. But I can certainly take you up there. There's not much to see, though, really. They're just docks."

"Still, I have to be thorough," said Kaitlyn. "Please? And I'd like to hear more about this pirate ghost."

"Alright, I'll tell you what; we'll take a run up there on my motorcycle and have a quick look. But I still need to play host to you, and since di island seems to have so many long lost visitors, I think tonight's just the right time for one of my world famous luaus," I said. "Of course, I always think it's the right time. But if I'm gonna do it, we better go now; lots to do all of a sudden."

There was indeed a lot to do; well, a few things, anyway. Okay, one. But that one thing could at times be damned difficult, especially on the days my uncle didn't want to be found. I hoped today wasn't one of those days, because if I was going to throw a decent luau, I was going to need to borrow his pirate P.A. system.

Chapter 7
"There's a pirate in di jungle."

My old Indian motorcycle seemed happy to be back on the road again, even if that road only went a few miles in every direction. I suppose it was the perfect retirement home for a bike; a nice place to still be useful without being asked to drive from New Jersey to Sturgis and back, and no winters to worry about. And as long as it promised not to play *throw the Jack as far as you can*, I was glad to take a break from walking.

I was also happy to have Kaitlyn's arms wrapped around me again for a while as we rode. I'd missed Isabella more than I could possibly express when she left me, but the loss had faded over time. Now that I had some human touch back in my life, I realized once more what I'd been missing.

As promised, I took Kaitlyn to the shipping docks on the northern end of di island, where she took a few pictures and asked some questions. I didn't see what was so interesting about a bunch of docks, but apparently it was part of her job. Maybe she was writing a chapter in a travel guide about di island and had to cover all the bases. Or like Zac Brown, she just wanted to get away to where the boat leaves from.

Afterwards, we rode to the start of the trail that went up to Black Dog's Peak, the hill where my uncle liked to watch the ships come in, and made the trek up it. I was hoping I'd find him at the top, but if he was around, he was staying out of sight.

"A nice view from up here," said Kaitlyn, shielding her eyes from the sun. The hill was the highest spot on our salty piece of land, and from it you could see di island in almost every direction, save the south side where a small grove of trees stood. "But what's that?" she asked, pointing.

"The reason we came up here," I said.

"Really? If I didn't know better, I'd say it looks like a cannon," said Kaitlyn. "Are you planning on sinking that go-fast boat that was roaring around di island this morning?"

"If I thought I could hit it, I might," I said, going over to the gun. "And if I had any ammunition with a bite."

I'd purchased the tiny cannon for Billy a few months ago, although most people thought I was nuts to arm him. It was heavily anchored to a brick and wood base that Jedidiah, di island carpenter, artist, and all around creator, had built to house it. It didn't have a ton of power, but when it went off, you could easily hear it from one shore to the other, and the porpoises out to sea likely wondered what the hell was going on, too. As I said though, there were no cannonballs, and it only fired blanks. I did know where to draw that line, even if it might already be farther out than it should be.

I walked around the cannon, examining it, and touching it as much as possible.

"What exactly are you doing?" said Kaitlyn, worriedly.

"I'm trying to figure out how to fire it," I said.

"Are you crazy?" said Kaitlyn. "That's a good way to get yourself killed."

"Aye, it is indeed, lass," said a familiar voice.

I turned, and found Uncle Captain Billy Black Dog standing there in full pirate regalia, replica flintlock in hand. I wasn't too surprised he'd appeared; he liked to skulk around out of sight watching me, and I figured messing with his cannon was a sure way to make him show himself. "Ahoy, Captain!" I said.

"Ahoy yerself, scallywag!" growled Billy. "Now step away from me cannon before I open fire on yer scurvy behind."

I did as I was told, carefully edging away towards Kaitlyn, who looked to be in need of some assurance she hadn't gone mad in the tropical heat. I wasn't worried about Billy hurting me, or anyone else for that matter; he hadn't harmed anything bigger than a lobster since I'd known him, but I liked to act my part in his pirate play.

"I'm just taking a wild guess here, but this wouldn't be the ghost of Captain Black Dog, would it?" said Kaitlyn, under her breath.

"The one and only," I said.

"And you say he's your uncle?" she said. "Or was, since he's dead or something?"

"Yes, and for more information, ask me later, or read the little booklet attached to our rum bottles," I said.

"So who's the wench?" said Billy.

"Wench?!" said Kaitlyn, defensively.

"From him, it's a term of endearment; it means he likes you," I said. "Captain, this be Kaitlyn Mars, a, er, scribe from England."

Kaitlyn looked at me, but I shook my head *forget it* at her.

"A scribe?" said Billy, sticking his pistol in his belt, evidently deciding Kaitlyn was harmless. "One of them brainy types, eh? What's she doin' with you, then, lad?"

I mentally counted to three, then said, "We came up here to see if we could borrow your cannon," I said.

"That explains why you're here, not why she's with you," said Billy. "Guess it doesn't matter, though; you'll screw it up with her like you always do. When he pisses ya off, lass, come and see me; I'll teach ya some livin' like a pirate maneuvers."

"You'll have to excuse him," I said. "I do, or at least try to."

"It's alright; I like him," said Kaitlyn, smiling.

"A lassie with excellent taste, so I still have to be askin' meself why she's lashed herself to you," said Billy, graciously. "Now what's this about you needin' my cannon? You wouldn't be havin' another of yer buccaneer beach balls tonight, would ye?"

"That's exactly what I'm doing, Captain," I said. "Could you help me out, and do an announcement to di islanders?"

"Aye, any chance to clear me guns is a welcome one," said Billy, happily. That was part of the deal; my uncle was only allowed to fire it for a reason, since I didn't want di island to start sounding like Michael Bay was filming here. And my parties were that usual reason. "You two need to clear out then; I won't be showin' ya where I keep my ordinance."

"That would be more information than we need to know anyway," I said. "Thanks, Captain Black Dog. And as always, you be welcome to join us at the festivities."

"I'll have to check me schedule; I think I'm supposed to be plunderin' Portugal tonight. But if I get done early, I'll try and make 'er," said Billy.

Kaitlyn and I waved goodbye to the ghost of Captain Black Dog, and scurried down the hill to safety. We waited by my motorcycle a few moments, trying to anticipate the coming noise, but it didn't help. With a incredibly sharp *"KA-BOOM!"* the cannon went off and we both jumped about three feet in the air; it was just one of those noises you can't prepare yourself for, like the kids screaming their lungs out in the checkout lanes at Walmart.

Now all we had to do was go back to my place on the beach and wait; everyone on di island would have heard the cannon blast, and if they'd happened to have their head inside a bucket or something, someone would tell them the party was on. Soon di islanders who wanted to attend would begin to show up to my hut, bringing eats and drinks, while I provided the location, my frozen concoctions, and a wee case of rum or two.

It was the perfect way to throw a party; you never knew who would show up, and what would be on the food and drink menu. Sometimes there'd be music, sometimes limbo, and sometimes a few tourons would even get wind of it and crash the festivities. And the best part was I got to play host without working my arse off to do so.

For the first time in a long while I wouldn't be going stag. And Crazy Chester would very likely be there, since he wasn't about to miss a party, and that always livened things up. And Marty? I doubted if he knew what he was in for.

Then again, *I* didn't know what I was in for either, because I'd never met Party Hardy Marty.

Like I said, you never knew who was going to show up.

Chapter 8
"Di Captain and di Captain."

You think ya know a guy.

Then he brings chicken to your party.

Which wouldn't have been all that bad, if he hadn't insisted the chick in question was his date.

Marty showed up to my tiki hut feeling, well, just a little bit festive. To put it another way, if Marty's mindset had been a city, it would have been New Orleans. Or more likely, given the live chicken under his arm, Key West. During Fantasy Fest. Under a full moon.

It hadn't taken him very long to unwind, which may have had to do with leaving him in the good hands of di islanders at Monkey Drool's. I doubted he'd built up much of a tolerance to Pickled Parrots and Toasted Toucans while playing family man either, so he'd been quick to take phlight with his newphound phriends. I wasn't sure where the chicken fit into everything, but he seemed to be in a pheathered state of mind.

"Is Marty always like that?" asked Kaitlyn, watching him madly dance around the fire to Boyd's bongos, chicken raised high to the sky. He looked like he was about to engage in some ancient island voodoo ritual.

"I admit I haven't seen him for a while, but I'd have to say this is probably a first," I said. "Still, I remember limboing around the beach wearing only my underwear, an eye patch, and a sombrero during one of my first nights here, so I'm not going to say anything. Di islands can do that to you. If you're lucky."

I watched as Marty pulled the chicken down close to him and gave it a big kiss on the beak.

"That's lucky?" said Kaitlyn.

"Maybe for the chicken," I said.

"I doubt she feels that way," said Kaitlyn.

"At least there was no tongue involved," I said.

"Buenos tardes, boss," said Ernesto. "Hello, Miss Kaitlyn."

"Hello, Ernesto," said Kaitlyn.

"You two already met, I see; you've really been making the rounds," I said. It was true; it seemed like everyone who'd shown up at the party already knew Kaitlyn. Then again, as friendly as di islanders were, I guess it shouldn't have been all that surprising.

"Si, I showed her all around the plantation," said Ernesto.

"It's very nice; Ernesto said you've been fixing it up for months. You could probably make it a tourist attraction, too," said Kaitlyn.

"Is that why you went there, to check out its rubberneck appeal?" I said. "You know, I still don't get exactly what it is you do for a living, besides drink on the beach. And I know you don't own a rum factory, so you can't have the same job as me."

"Like I said, I check everything out about a place for potential visitors; safety, beauty, amenities, shopping, attractions, etc, etc," said Kaitlyn. "That's all I can say; the rest is top secret."

I shrugged. "Fine, be that way. Can you at least tell me how we're we rating so far?" I said.

"Very high," said Kaitlyn. "Di island is for the most part unspoiled, and definitely beautiful. The people are warm and friendly, it's safe, and there are just enough things to see and do."

"That's my island," I said.

"I'm going to dance with your girlfriend, now," said Marty, appearing suddenly behind me.

"What happened to your date?" I asked.

"I put her down to get a fresh drink, and she ran off into the woods," said Marty, sadly. "Not the first time it's ever happened. So do I have permission?"

"From me, yes; I can't speak for Kaitlyn," I said.

"As long as you promise not to try and hold me above your head or kiss me on the beak," said Kaitlyn. "Let's go."

I watched the two of them head over to the dance floor, or at least to the plot of sand that always ended up being the mambo spot, then I walked over to talk to Crazy Chester and Jolly Roger. "You seem pretty uncrazy this evening," I said to Chester. "What's going on?"

"It's because *he's* in there," said Chester, glaring at the woods behind my hut through narrowly slitted eyes.

"Who's in der, mon?" asked Roger, casting his gaze in the same direction.

"*He* is," said Chester, italicizing the he yet again.

I looked too, but didn't see anyone either. "Maybe you are just as crazy as usual after all," I said. "There's no one there."

"You wanna bet?" said Chester. "You! In the woods; we know you're in there. Show yourself!"

"What's this *we* stuff?" I asked, doing some italicizing of my own. But as I watched, a shady figure emerged slowly from the trees. It moved towards us through the shadows, then stepped into the full moonlight.

"Uncle Billy! I mean, Captain Black Dog," I said.

"Aye, the captain be present. The question is though, what's this bilge rat doin' here?" said Billy, gruffly.

"Me?" said Chester. "If anyone's a varmint around here, it's you, Black Dog."

Billy took a step forward, and said, "Ha! That's a good one, comin' from a no good thievin' kidnappin' landlubber like yourself."

"I'm not a landlubber, and you know it!" argued Chester, moving closer as well. "Take that back!"

"Alright! You're not a landlubber; ya do captain that Lazy Lizard of yers. And it's a fine ship, I admit," admitted Billy. "But yer still a thief!"

"I am not, but you are," said Chester.

Billy puffed his chest out and pointed at it. "Pirate!" he said.

"Fine, I'll give ya that one back; but *I'm* still not a thief," said Chester.

The two captains finally stopped inching towards one another, since they were about to bump noses, while a small crowd of party guests gathered around them to see what all the fuss was about. I didn't know what the hell was going on with my uncle and Chester, but I decided it was time to find out.

"Parlay!" I announced, simultaneously giving the universal T timeout signal with my hands.

"You can't claim the right of parlay, lad; this ain't your fight," said Billy.

"Au contraire," I said. "You two are on my land, and as lord of this, er, sand, I have the right to know what's going on."

"Arrr!" said Billy in protest. "Damn the French! I'll tell ya, then, but he's just gonna deny it like always. This lecherous, low down, scurvy scoundrel stole my first mate!"

Chester sighed. "I keep telling you, I didn't steal him; I have no idea what happened to him."

"First mate?" I said, wondering who they might be talking about. Then it occurred to me. "You mean Sam?"

"Aye," said Billy.

Sam was my uncle's black lab. I'd given him to Billy a couple of years ago, to replace the dog he'd lost during the shipwreck that started his whole pirate ghost persona. "What does Sam have to do with anything?" I asked.

"Because the last time I saw him, a couple of months ago, he was down by the docks, hanging around this blaggard," said Billy, sadly. "After that, he was gone, and so was Chester."

"I didn't even know Sam was missing," I said.

"Jack, if everything you didn't know suddenly turned into rum, I'd be a happy, drownin', man," said Billy.

"Thanks, as always," I said.

"Yer welcome," said Billy. "All I know is, Captain Crazy here has always been too buddy buddy with my mate, and I could tell he was hopin' to steal him for his own crew. I'm damned sure Sam refused, and the fool kidnapped him and took him to his fortress in the evil kingdom..."

"...and now every time I come to di island, he keeps stealin' things off my boat!" complained Chester.

Billy pointed at his chest again. "Pirate!"

"That's not an excuse for everything, dang it!" said Chester. "But yeah, I liked Sam; he was a good dog, er, sea dog. And that day, I was feeding him some beef jerky I had on my boat, giving him a treat like I always did. But I didn't take him with me!"

"Liar," said Billy.

"Well, how are we going to settle this?" I said.

"If you'd have procured me a cutlass like I've been askin', I'd have settled it a long time ago," said Billy.

"One of the many reason I haven't," I said. I thought about it. "I propose a treaty; we'll all look into it, put the news out on the Coconut Telegraph that Sam's missing, and see what we can find out. Until then, you two cease all hostilities. Agreed?"

"Yes," said Chester.

Billy stroked his goatee thoughtfully. "Does that include plunderin' his stuff?" he asked.

"Yes!" I said. *"All* hostilities."

"Damn! Fine, I agree; for now," said Billy. "But I ain't gonna enjoy it."

"Then go drink some rum," I said, pointing at the tiki bar.

"That I will enjoy," said Billy, wandering off to do so after giving Chester one last dirty look.

"I thought you might," I said after him.

"Any advice for me?" said Chester.

"Go drink some rum," I said, pointing at the tiki bar.

"Do you ever prescribe anything else?" said Chester.

"Nope. In fact, I'm telling myself right now to go drink some rum with you," I said, putting my arm around Chester's shoulder and guiding him towards the tiki bar.

"And then what?" asked Chester.

"Then, we wait and see what happens next like always," I said. "Because you just never know."

I never did know what was going to happen from one moment on di island to the next. Usually it was nothing extraordinary, which was fine by me. What *was* extraordinary and freeing was not having what was likely to occur during any given moment in your life already determined by a schedule, like in the old, dark times. Five days of work, two potential days of fun. Between sleeping, getting up at a certain time, driving to work, and all the hours locked in my cubicle, roughly sixty percent of my life had been prearranged. No wonder people sometimes feel their life is stuck in a rut; it often is, following the same, deep, tire tracks that had been made the week before.

Then again, life is also good at throwing the proverbial banana peel down in your path no matter where you are, and the world you know can go flying out from under your feet in a heartbeat. I should have been watching my step even though I was living on di island, because it turns out beach sand isn't any softer than concrete if you land on your ass hard enough.

Chapter 9
"This new hotel's not alright with me."

My luau that evening ended up slowly winding down into a small sit around the fire and swap stories affair, which was fine. Every party was like a living being and you had to accept them for who they were, and they all seemed to have a moment of truth in their life that would determine their personality for the rest of the night.

On this occasion, the confrontation between the two crabby sailors had mellowed things out, despite the best efforts of Marty, who made a stab at squeezing ten years of missed revelry into one evening. After several hours of flirting, skinny dipping, and Day-O singing, he eventually passed out in my hammock, where he slept until way past noon before trying to stand up and focus. Luckily for him I knew he'd need a Bloody Mary, so all he had to do was stumble on over to the tiki bar.

A week later Marty still seemed to be in a state of total denial. He never mentioned anything to do with his life and family back on the mainland, and it was almost as if his memories before arriving had been erased. I kept waiting for something to snap him out of it so I wouldn't have to get involved, but he remained a happy zombiefied island convert. I decided to give it just a few more days, and then reluctantly perform a ritual of my own to try and break his trance.

Amazingly enough, Kaitlyn and I were also still in our own little hypnotic state of getting along way too well for our own good. What shocked me the most was that I hadn't really even tried to make it happen; it just did. I'd loved Isabella, but it was like a gambling trip to Vegas, and I never knew when I was going to crap out and go bust. And dating Brittany had been like a vacation in Orlando; sometimes fun, but tiring, and there was always something waiting to piss me off.

But being with Kaitlyn was like a day on the beach. We just were, and I didn't spend any time thinking about what we were doing. To steal a phrase, it was just a peaceful, easy feeling, and I was enjoying it, even if I didn't know how long it was going to last.

So when I woke up that late morning as usual and walked out onto my porch as usual I was in a great mood, which was also as usual. The sun was shining, the breeze was breezing, the palms were rustling, and the waves were lapping. Nothing was out of the ordinary, except for the two men in my yard, dressed in pin striped suits. They were busily pointing and talking and ruining my overall view of my beach, as if a portal had opened in hell and a couple of evil corporate guru's from Image Makers had fallen through it into my paradise.

I rubbed my eyes and gave my cheek a light slap to make sure I wasn't having another of my flashback nightmares, then padded slowly across the sand towards the men. One of them saw my approach and alerted the other, and they stood waiting at attention in a neat line until my lazy arrival.

"If you guys are with the CIA, Crazy Chester left this morning," I said.

The man holding the clipboard looked at me, and then at his partner, and said. "No, sir; we're not with the CIA."

"Then can you tell me what you're doing on my land?" I asked. "Besides being terribly overdressed for beach combing?"

"Your land?" asked the one wearing the mini cellphone headset above his ear.

"Yeah; I live here. It may not look like much to you, but it's my home," I said, indicating my shack.

"Ah, then you must be Jack Danielson," said clipboard.

"I don't know if I must be, but I am," I said, wishing I was awake enough to wonder why someone standing on my beach in a three piece suit knew who I was. "And it's early, at least in my world, so why don't you just tell me what you want so I can get on with my daily slacking."

Clipboard looked puzzled. "Hasn't anyone from di island been in contact with you in the last few days?" he said.

"We don't get *in contact* with one another here; we just meet up and talk. But no one has mentioned anything out of the ordinary to me, no. What the hell's going on, anyway?" I said. "Who are you guys?"

"Well, I wish Mr. Wonbago would have talked to you like he said he was going to, because we want this to be as amicable as possible and didn't intend it to be a surprise," said headset. "You're an important man on di island, and we're looking forward to working closely with you."

I didn't like the sound of the variations of the words *work* or *close*. "Yeah, they tell me I'm the big kahuna, or something," I said. "And normally I like surprises, but I'm getting the feeling I'm not going to like this one."

"It's nothing bad, I assure you. In fact, it'll be very good for your rum factory and di island," said headset. "But I'm afraid you are going to have to vacate these premises. We'll give you a few days to do so of course, but..."

"What?!" I said. "Like hell, I will; I'm not going anywhere. This is my property."

"Actually, no, it's not; it's ours," said headset, too damned calmly for my liking. "The sale was finalized two days ago. And from what I understand, this never was your land."

"That's ridiculous. I-," I started, then paused as my brain pulled up some files on the subject. Now that I thought about it, I'd just gone in and talked to Mr. Wonbago way back when, and he'd said it was okay for me to live here since no one else was at the time. Di island had been so casual about everything since my arrival that I'd more or less assumed it meant that the place was now mine, but if they actually had any kind of property laws...

"If you'd like, we could go to the bank and Mr. Wonbago can show you the papers," said clipboard. "It's all perfectly legal."

"I don't believe this," I said. "So explain the part where this is a good thing. And I'll ask you one more time; who the hell are you?"

Clipboard took out a business card and handed it to me. "We're with Anderton Hotel Properties Unlimited; this part of di island is the future site of our newest venture, *The Winslow,* a super premium luxury resort," he said, proudly. "Your hut sits roughly where the dolphin shaped pool will be."

"You guys are crazy, but that's what you get for running around in this heat in those suits," I said. "In the first place, no one's building anything here, unless it's my barbecue grill and fire pit. And second, even *if*

I'd allow it to happen, di island doesn't have the kind of infrastructure a resort like you're talking about would need; we don't even have paved roads."

"Yet," said headset. "Just another reason you should be pleased; we'll be bringing you tarred roads, an upgraded power plant, better plumbing...there's even talk of a small airport one day for private planes to land."

"Yeah, full of snobby, rich, assholes," I said. "I bet even Mr. Strickland will come and torment me. I mean, how much is it going to cost to stay at this little *Winslow* of yours?"

"We're not sure, but an early ballpark figure would be about a thousand dollars a night," said clipboard. "That's for a room facing the woods; for an ocean view, it would be more, of course."

"Of course. And if I'm lucky, Brittany and her daddy will come and see me now, too," I said. "And you think you're going to get away with this?"

Headset shrugged. "I don't really see what you or anyone else can do about it," he said. "And I am surprised you're so upset. Not to mention that you didn't seem to know a thing about it."

"How would I?" I said. "I evidently missed the board meeting with Wonbago."

"But I would have thought Ms. Kaitlyn Mars would have said something; that is why she was here," said clipboard.

"You want to run that last part by me again?" I said, trying not to hyperventilate.

"We hired Kaitlyn's firm for one last check of di island; we've had our eye on putting a property here for a year or so, but we'd heard the place had been changing, and wanted to make sure it still met with Anderton's high standards," said clipboard.

"And Kaitlyn confirmed that for you, did she?" I said.

"Yes, and she did a very thorough job," said headset. "We were very pleased with her work. She didn't tell you what she was doing?"

"Not precisely, no," I said, evenly.

"Well, she was probably trying to protect our interests; we were worried someone else might swoop in at the last second and buy up the property before we committed. I can understand some of your concerns, then, not having all the facts," said headset. "But believe me, it will be for the best. You stand to make more money, as do di islanders, and di island itself will soon be much more modern and civilized, instead of the quaint, but backwards place it is now."

That may have been what headset had said to me, but what I'd heard was, *"Resistance is futile; you will be assimilated!"*

"We'll see about that; in fact, we'll see about a lot of things!" I said, stomping off to go get cleaned up, call someone on the phone I didn't have, scream at the ocean, smack Wonbago in the head, find a phaser to chase these two Borg off my property, and above all, find Kaitlyn.

"Resistance is futile!" clipboard shouted after me.

Chapter 10
"Trying to reason with Wonbago season."

I found Wonbago first; it wasn't difficult, since as usual, he was at the bank slash post office slash every other kind of office located in the Crossroads. I walked straight into his office, and slammed the door shut behind me.

"We need to talk," I said, angrily.

"Do you have an appointment, mon?" he said, ever the non-rattled bureaucrat.

"Cut the crap; I'm not making an appointment just to talk to you," I said.

"If you insist," Wonbago said. "I just wanted to find out which official jacket to wear."

"I don't know. Do you have a sneaky bastard coat?" I said.

"No, that one I do not," said Wonbago.

"You might want to go get a fitting. And I'm talking about the resort, and you know it. What did you do, decide to make some profit behind everyone's back? Did you just sell off that part of di island for a nice chunk of change for your offshore account?" I said. "Then again, this bank *is* technically offshore, so you would have been all set."

"Actually, dat land was owned by no one, so di money will be divided between all di islanders," said Wonbago calmly, nonplussed by my accusations.

"Oh," I said, feeling a bit like an idiot for not the first time in my life. "Sorry. But still, was there any discussion about who to sell the land to? Maybe I would have bought it."

"I don't tink you have di kind of money dey agreed to, mon," said Wonbago.

"How do you know?" I said. "How much was it?"

Wonbago picked up a pen and wrote something on his notepad, drawing a lot of loops, then tore it off and slid it towards me. It was a number with so many zeros that it looked like an offer from the New York Yankees.

"That much, huh?" I said.

"Yes," said Wonbago. "And I am in charge of di unowned property here on di island, which means it is my job to do what is best with it."

"But this isn't what's best," I argued. "This is going to change di island forever."

"Dat be di point," said Wonbago.

I decided not to argue further; I knew Wonbago well enough to know that he was stubborn as hell, and that I wasn't going to change his mind alone. And I'd always had the feeling he'd simply tolerated me as an outsider, someone who'd been a means to an end to get the factory running.

"Well, is the sale final? I know headset said it was, but is there any way it could still be reversed?" I asked.

"Der is no way they can stop it now, if dat's what you mean," said Wonbago.

"No, I mean, if the Anderton Company turned out to be evil aliens from the planet Crouton, and you found out they planned to turn all di islanders into salad fixings and serve them at the Winslow, could *you* still stop it? *If* you wanted to?" I said.

"Yes, I could," said Wonbago. "Di sale can be canceled for a week. But I don't tink it be likely dey be aliens, mon."

Wonbago was a master of defensive sarcasm, bouncing it right back at ya like a spiked beach volleyball rejected into your face. But it didn't matter; I'd found out what I needed to know. At least I still had time to figure everything out and come up with a plan, and maybe get this monstrosity aborted before it was too late for everyone.

I'd never been much for causes, but I'd found one now; Jimmy had helped the Gulf Coast after Katrina's attack, and now I had to save di island from the invasion of the rich and famous whether it liked it or not. And if that meant lying down in front of a bulldozer or two, so be it.

At least it would be on the beach. And with my portable Margaritaville Frozen Concoction Maker, I could hold out for days, if necessary.

Until one of our batteries gave out, anyway.

Chapter 11
"Lookin' for a smart woman in an undercover skirt."

As a wise man once said, love stinks.

Not the actual love itself, of course; that part is wonderful. But the trying to get it and keep it and the whole relationship deal, that can be hell.

Love is like golf, actually. For one thing, it can be very expensive. There's usually a lot of swearing involved, and drinking can make it less painful. After you're done with a bad round or relationship you swear you're never going to play the stupid game again, even though you know it's not true. Because when you hit that perfect shot or have that perfect moment with someone, it makes it all worthwhile for some asinine reason.

In my case, I'd been having that perfect round with Kaitlyn. My swing had been smooth and effortless, and I'd managed to hit every fairway and green in regulation. And now all of a sudden I found myself standing in the bottom of a pot hole bunker that was deep enough to make any tour pro wet himself, wondering what the hell I'd done to deserve my predicament this time.

I didn't even feel like trying to chip out; my instincts were to just break my club over my knee and walk off the course. But either way I knew I had to talk to Kaitlyn first, and today, since she was leaving di island tomorrow.

I found her walking down Coconut Lane towards the Crossroads, which was good since there were no islanders around to eavesdrop, an island pastime. We both stopped about ten paces apart like gunfighters, and stood waiting for one another to break the silence.

"You heard?" said Kaitlyn.

"How can you tell?" I said. "Oh wait, probably by the fact that all my belongings are hanging from the proverbial stick slung over my shoulder. I've lost the beach part of my bum in just a few short hours."

"You could always live at the plantation," Kaitlyn suggested tenuously.

"Two Minnesotans is a crowd, and Ernesto would have me at his mercy," I said. "Besides, I *liked* my beach."

"I'm sorry," said Kaitlyn. "I was just doing my job."

"You could have at least told me," I said.

"It wouldn't have done any good; unless I lied on my report, they were pretty likely to go ahead with their plans," said Kaitlyn.

"And I suppose you think lying to them would have been out of the question," I said. "Have you looked around? I mean, I thought that's what your job was, wasn't it? Di island is perfect the way it is. Never mind the fact that my little hut is a goner; you know this hotel is going to ruin the place. It'll never be the same again; it'll just be one more spot on the map that's been civilized to death."

"I understand that; I really do. I love di island, too, and I've only been here a short time. Why do you think I was planning on coming back so soon?" said Kaitlyn, and I looked at her. "Besides to see you. But what was I supposed to do? What would you have done?"

"In the old, dark days, or now, after I've liberated myself from me?" I said. "Now, I'd have done anything to keep this place the way it is."

"Is that why you went ahead and opened the rum factory? Because I guarantee that changed di island, too," argued Kaitlyn.

She had a valid point, but I wasn't about to acknowledge its existence. "But di islanders wanted me to do that; I damn near didn't have any choice," I said. "Besides, that was rum! This is building a place for annoying, pompous, self absorbed, better than anyone else rich people to come and try and get away from it all. Di island's gonna be overrun with them. I'd personally rather suffer a plague of locusts."

"How do you know di islanders don't want this, too? Just like they wanted you to open the factory to make their lives a little better?" said Kaitlyn.

"Come on; how could they?" I said. "And even if they did, I'm not sure they'd really know what the consequences are going to be. Most of them haven't lived in *civilization*. They don't know how good they've got it just the way things are."

"That's your opinion; did you ask any of them?" said Kaitlyn. "Take the time to find out what they think?"

"Wonbago, yeah; but he doesn't count. He's the government, financial system, and every other kind of bureaucracy all rolled into one," I said. "Other than that, I've only known they were going to pave paradise for a few hours now, so I haven't had time to poll my constituents."

"Well, maybe you should," said Kaitlyn. "I just left a bunch of people sitting at Monkey Drool's; you should go and talk to them."

"Fine, I will," I said. I closed the ten paces between us and was going to walk petulantly right past Kaitlyn, when she reached out and grabbed my arm.

"Again, I'm sorry. That's all I can say. I'll be around until tomorrow morning, and you have my number if you ever want to get a hold of me after that," she said, leaning forward and speaking quietly into my ear. She kissed me lightly on the cheek, and added, "If you ever get a phone." Then she let go of my arm and continued walking towards the Crossroads.

I turned my head and watched her go for a moment, then headed towards the Monkey.

Chapter 12
"Di pirate conspiracy."

Kaitlyn hadn't been lying (about this, anyway; okay, about anything, technically), and I found quite a good sized crowd out back at Monkey Drool's. There was a lively, buzzing, conversation going on, which gave me the feeling the coconut telegraph had been doing its job once again.

I stopped first at the bar and got a Kalik from the Innkeeper. I needed a drink, which was rare these days; usually when I had one I just wanted one. Then I went over and sat in the open seat next to Roger at the big, long table in the center of the sand, and said, "Well?"

"Well what, mon?" asked Roger.

"Well, you know what, what. And don't try to plead ignorant; you probably all knew about it before I did," I said.

"Do you mean about di new resort, boss?" asked Faith.

"Yeah, that's exactly what I mean," I said. "I'm almost afraid to ask what you think; there are too many happy faces around the table."

"Yours doesn't seem to be in attendance," said Roger.

"You're damned right it's not," I said. "But I see yours is. Of course, seeing as how you're Jolly Roger, that doesn't necessarily mean anything."

"This time it be all good, mon," said Roger, widening his grin. "More passengers for di ferry, more people to meet, and more electricity; maybe I can have air conditioning now."

"I see; Ernesto? Do you feel the same way?" I asked.

"Si, it will be good to have a real road, for one thing. I've always wanted to own a car again, ever since I left Mexico. I suppose I always could have, but something about pavement makes me want one now even more," said Ernesto.

I shuddered. "A car, eh? My motorcycle is feisty enough as it is. I remember what it was like owning a real, modern, state of the art automobile with the hypochondriac chips installed that tell the warning lights when to light up so you can go give money to a mechanic. No thank you. And you Faith? What's your take? You're always talking about keeping things simple; back me up here."

"No can do, boss; I'm happy making di rum, and keeping dat simple. But der are still a lot of people who would like another place to work, and I'll be happy for dem when dey get it," said Faith.

I sighed. "And I'm sure you agree with all this modernizing, too, Cavin."

"Actually, I don't," said Cavin. "I come from California, remember? The last thing I want is for di island to turn into mini-Los Angeles."

"Exactly!" I said, happy to find an ally at last, even if it was one who was exaggerating. "I was beginning to think I was the only person who felt that way."

Cavin shook his head. "Boyd and Pat just left here; neither of them were happy, either. Pat was so upset I thought he was going to start crying in his Labatts."

I cringed. "We still gotta break him of his hoser *only Canadian beer is good beer* routine," I said. "I'd cry in my Labatt's if that's what was in front of me, too. But I know how he feels, even though he stands to gain from the resort being here, too. Do we have anyone else on our side?"

"Me," said Gus, sitting down.

"When did you get here?" I asked.

"About three hours ago. Is it okay with you if I get up from the table occasionally to pee?" said Gus. "And you took my chair, by the way."

"Sorry," I said.

"We've got more important things to worry about; there's no damned way I'm gonna let di island turn into another tourist trap," growled Gus. "I'm running out of places to get away from it all, and I ain't gonna give this one over to a bunch of Fortune 500 CEOs and their plastic wives."

"So what are we gonna do about it?" I said.

Gus looked around the table suspiciously. "We can't talk here; do you still have rum at your place?"

"I always have rum at my place; I just don't know how long it will have my place to be at," I said.

"Then let's go," said Gus, standing up.

"But I just got here!" I said.

"Can't be helped; too many pro-Winslow ears around here," said Gus. "Come on, Cavin, and anyone else who thinks this resort is about as good an idea as light beer."

"If we're going to have a meeting, shouldn't we tell the others? Pat and Boyd, for instance?" I said, rising from my chair and preparing for yet another trip across di island.

"I've already got it covered; the troops are mustering at ground zero as we speak," said Gus.

"How did you know to send them to my place?" I said.

"Where else can we get free rum?" said Gus. "And you can't plot a little pirate anarchy without a healthy supply of rum."

"We could have used Crazy Chester if we're serious about this," I said. "If anyone knows how to disrupt the onslaught of civilization, it's probably him."

"He's on his way back; I buzzed him in my plane earlier and radioed an SOS," said Gus.

"Don't you mean an SOI?" I asked. "Save our island?"

"No, then it would it be an SDI," said Cavin. "Save DI island."

"Just move it you two, or we're all gonna end up SOL," said Gus. "Shit out of luck."

Chapter 13
"We pushed di fool button."

"No, no, no; you've got to lean it against the wall more," said Pat, softly.

"I'm trying," whispered Cavin. "It's not easy; the bucket is too big."

"I told Gus we needed a smaller one, but he wouldn't listen," said Pat. "He said there'd be a bigger splash this way."

"Yeah, on me, not them," complained Cavin.

"Would you two just hurry up?" I hissed, looking around the dark room nervously. "They're liable to come back soon, and I don't want to end up sitting in the jail we don't have."

It was a week after our declaration of hostilities against Anderton Properties, and the war was going badly.

Our opening cannon salvo had been a series of threats of legal actions, PR campaigns, deportation schemes, and finding a way to buy the land ourselves. None of it had even come close to being effective, and we were repeatedly blocked by Wonbago and petty things like international trade and real estate laws, as well as a lack of any real cash to speak of, at least not enough to put a dent in a hull as mighty as theirs. So we had been soon forced to switch tactics.

I'm not sure what you would call the second wave of our attacks, besides deluded, if we really believed they were going to do any good. Childish and stupid also came to mind as possible monikers, but desperate times called for asinine measures, and we were up to the task.

Which was why the three of us were currently sneaking around in the dark of headset's room at the Coconut Motel, having climbed in through the window, none of which had locks to keep us out. And why Cavin was struggling to balance the giant bucket of goat's milk on the bathroom door, just so.

It was another in a series of lame retributions that wasn't likely to accomplish much of anything, except perhaps to make us feel better. We didn't seem to have a General Patton in our midst, who would have come up with something better than letting *Pepe Di Evil One* loose in the office headset and clipboard were using at the bank. Pepe was a rooster with a just plain bad attitude; he liked to terrorize me, that was for sure, and I had the flip-flop protected toe scars to prove it. But he probably wasn't going to scare an entire corporation of di island. And neither was the ghost of Captain Billy Black Dog, oooing and oooahing outside their window at midnight, while growling out pirate curses. But I do think the laxative that I happened to somehow spill into their rum samples when they were touring the factory was a stroke of near genius. I only hope the Japanese tourists that had the misfortune of being in their tour group didn't hold it against us.

Yes, it was stupid, and maybe we couldn't actually annoy the Anderton people off di island, but it wasn't going to stop us from trying.

"Got it," said Cavin, after what seemed like an eternity had passed.

"Good; climb out the bathroom window, and we'll meet you outside," said Pat.

"Better split up and meet back at headquarters, instead," said Cavin.

"Fine, whatever; let's just get the hell out of here," I said, anxious to get this over with. There was far more tension in the air than I was used to, and I wasn't enjoying being reminded that I still had nerves to be nervous with after all. I clumsily clambered out the window, landing in the soft sand under it with a thud, then picked myself up and non-nonchalantly (as well as I could) meandered back to my place for our nightly strategy session.

And an hour later, almost wished I was back in the motel room where I'd been safe(r).

"Sippers," said Pat, and he passed the glass down to me.

I took a sip of rum, then passed the glass over to Cavin. "Sippers," I said as well, leery of starting a battle at sea.

Cavin took a sip, then said, "Gulpers," and passed the glass back to me.

I took a big gulp, passed it to Gus, and said, "Sippers."

"Wuss," said Gus. "And if you think taking it easy on me means I'm gonna take it easy on ya back, then you don't know me at all, boyo." Gus took his sip, then handed it back to me. "Sandy bottoms."

We'd been playing a drinking game Gus had invented based on an old Royal Navy tradition. Sailors used to give a portion of their rum ration to a shipmate on their birthday, or for whatever reason they were feeling generous with their sugary gold. The amount they agreed to donate was designated either a sip, a gulp, or in my case...

I sighed and took the glass and finished it off. Luckily for my head and liver we'd sipped and gulped it down to the point where my sandy bottom, or full ration, was only about half of what it might have been. But it was more than adequate to give me a good keel hauling.

After recovering from the sting and slap of the rum, I said, "I don't see how this is helping."

"Neither do I," said Gus.

"You're the one who suggested it!" said Pat.

"Yeah, but I never said it was going to solve anything," said Gus.

"Then I think that's about enough of that," I said, feeling the universe spinning around me more than usual; it seemed when you got tipsy enough, you became very sensitive to physics.

"Double wuss," said Gus.

"No, I just wanna sit here and enjoy the rum I already have in me before sending any more down there; it would just get lost in the crowd, or worse yet, expelled from my property for exceeding the fire code occupancy limit," I said.

"Well, my body's philosophy when it comes to rum is, the more the merrier," said Gus. "Besides, I was just trying to get us in the proper frame of mind."

"You mean, whacked out of our heads?" said Boyd.

"If that's what it's gonna take to come up with a good idea of how to win this war, then yeah," said Gus. "And the best way to think out of the box is to not be able to think normally."

"Then you should be the next Einstein," said Pat.

"Thanks," said Gus. "I try."

At least it was another gorgeous night on my beach, even if those nights were numbered. We'd dragged my lawn chairs right down to the ocean's edge and set them up in a straight line facing the water, and every few seconds a fresh wave ran onto land and across my bare toes before rushing back out to sea. The moon was hanging just above the horizon, sending a path of twinkling lights towards us, sailing atop the calm waves. But as usual, it was the scent of the salty evening air that really told me where I was; nothing smells quite like the ocean. If they could realistically bottle the scent, I'd buy a whole cask. That is, if I didn't already have the real thing within my nostril's reach to tickle my olfactory fancies.

Which brought me back to the problem, which was that if our war continued on its present course of ineptitude, I wouldn't be allowed to sit where I was smelling without first renting a room. Which was also supposedly why we were lined up once again like a group of navy seals who'd landed on the beach, ready to defend it against all potential aggressors.

Our special forces unit was small, but what we lacked in numbers, we more than made up for with a certain zany, bad movie comedy something. There was myself, Gus, Cavin, Pat, Boyd, Marty, Crazy Chester, and Captain Billy Black Dog. I wanted to call our group the Magnificent Seven, which showed how well I could count, and thus we unfortunately became the Oddball Eight instead.

"Is it even worth it to keep trying to stop these guys?" I said. "If there's only seven of us-"

"Eight," said everyone else together, in a chorus of correctness.

"Fine, eight," I said. "My point is, that means everyone else on di island wants this hotel to be built; we're a bit outnumbered."

"So? They were outnumbered at the Alamo, too," said Pat.

"Yeah, and everyone died," said Gus.

"But they were remembered, at least," said Pat. "I'm Canadian, and even we heard about it."

"Because they had a good catchphrase," said Marty.

"That can be your department then, since you're the advertising expert," said Boyd. "Just in case we fail; like Pat said, it would be nice to be remembered."

"I'll see what I can come up with," said Marty.

"If we keep screwing up like we are, no one's gonna forget, believe me," said Gus.

Chester stood, and walked over to a position in front of us, which meant he was knee deep in the water. "Then I think it's time we escalated the battle; we ain't getting anywhere like this, and failure isn't an option."

Billy stood up and walked over to where Chester was addressing us from, and I thought maybe their feud was going to erupt again. But instead, he put his hand on Chester's shoulder.

"I agree with Captain Crazy," he said. "Even if he didn't bring Sam back yet and we haven't found him, which makes him a lying scoundrel. But we need to forget our differences and combine our forces against our common enemy; the East India Trading Company!"

"I thought that was what we've been doing," said Boyd.

"You think dowsing them with milk is gonna win this war?" said Chester.

"It was your idea!" said Cavin.

"I just thought it'd be fun," said Chester.

"Well, what else can we do?" said Pat.

"What else, can ye do?!" exclaimed Billy. "You should be askin' yerself what else *can't* ye do. What are ye, anyway; men or pirates?"

"Do we have to choose between the two?" asked Marty.

"What are you getting at, Captain?" I asked, before things got more out of control.

"We need to get down to specifics, and use everything we've got against them, 'cuz we all have special skills and resources. Jack, for instance; what could he do to help keep these blaggards from buildin' a stronghold on di island?" asked Billy.

"How 'bout burning down the rum factory?" suggested Chester.

"What?!" I yelped. "If you think I'm burning down my factory..."

"Not bad," said Gus. "It is the main tourist attraction here. Not to mention the fact that having our own official island rum puts us up with the bigger boys and makes us almost snooty, and a natural for a highbrow resort. As for me, I'd stop flying people to and from di island in a heartbeat, if it would help."

"Now wait a minute," I said. *If* I burned down my factory, which I won't do, you should have to crash your plane."

"Tough to do unless I'm flying it at the time," said Gus. "So unless you want to be in your factory when we set it on fire, I'll just say no to that one."

"Here's another thought," said Cavin. "Chester, do you remember saying people should be glad you even wear pants? Well, what if..."

"Now *that's* a good idea," said Chester, evilly.

"No, it's not!" I said.

"And I bet havin' a barrage of cannon fire all night long might keep those evil nobles from gettin' much sleep," said Billy.

"And neither is...okay, that one's not bad," I admitted. "But Chester needs to keep his bottoms on."

Chester frowned at me.

"What about Roger's boat?" said Gus.

I looked at Gus suspiciously. "What about it?"

"It'd be tough for anyone to get here without me *and* his ferry," said Gus.

"Jolly Roger's for the hotel, though, so he's not liable to stop transporting people," said Cavin.

"He might not want to, but if the Crustacean suddenly sprung a hole or two..." said Gus.

"I hope you're not suggesting what I think you're suggesting," said Pat.

"Collateral damage," said Gus.

"Alright, that's enough!" I snapped, and jumped to my feet. I instantly regretted it, as the world beneath me fired off a rum powered extra rotation or two. Once the Earth's orbit stabilized, I continued. "You guys should be ashamed of yourselves."

"You don't really think I was serious, do you?" said Gus. "I love Roger; I'd never do anything to hurt the man."

I sighed. "I don't know; it's hard to tell with you sometimes. I suppose you weren't, though," I said. "But it doesn't matter. *I'm* ashamed of myself."

"Why? Just because you don't want some luxury resort moving in here?" asked Pat.

"No, there's nothing wrong with not liking it," I said. "But to even think about trying to keep it from happening; that's just wrong. And selfish."

"You better es'plain yourself, Lucy," said Gus.

"Look, I never knew my dream was to live on a tropical island *and* own a rum factory; you just never even imagine something like that. It just happened. But I'd hate to lose it, now," I said. "And you with your plane, Gus, and Pat with his sporting goods store, Chester with his bar in the Keys, Boyd with his laid back, odd jobs lifestyle, even Black Dog and his piratitude..."

"What are you getting' at, lad?" asked Billy.

"We all pretty much have what we want in life; it may not be perfect, but it's pretty damned close to our dreams. Di islanders; if they want something more than they have, why the hell have we been trying to get in the way?" I said. "They're our friends, and just because we've moved here, been accepted by them, and consider ourselves islanders too, now, doesn't give us the right to try and regulate their lives. In fact, we should be happy for them, even if it might mess up our own little worlds."

"Why don't you tell us how you really feel?" said Gus.

"I guess I just did; it just took me a while to figure it out," I said. "Yeah, di island will never be the same, but I think we need to accept it."

"That, and there's probably nothing we could really do about it anyway," said Boyd.

"Although I think the pants thing might have worked," said Gus.

"Thanks," said Chester.

"So that's it then? We just sit back and let human nature take its course?" said Cavin.

"Yeah, I think so," I said. "It's time to run up the white flag."

"Oh, well," said Gus. "Should be a lot of rich broads hanging around Monkey Drool's; maybe I can retire early."

"I suppose I should put together a bid for their sport supplies," said Pat.

"Henri's gonna be happy, too; business was tough, but he should be fine, now," said Boyd.

"Maybe it's all for the best, after all," said Marty.

"Yeah," I said, quietly. "For the best."

Though it was hard to really feel that way. I was going to have to force myself to feel glad for my fellow islanders, even though I knew that getting out of the way was probably the right thing to do. And thinking all of this progress really began with my opening of the rum factory made me almost wish I'd never done so; I was going to miss di island that I'd come to know and love.

But what the hell. I was going to love her even if she was growing up.

Because she was my home, and that was one thing that was never going to change.

Chapter 14
"My friend is singing, vaya con dios."

I woke up the next morning feeling absolutely grand, a lot of which was in comparison to my mood the day before. Southern warmth feels a whole lot better traveling away from a Minnesota winter than a summer, for instance, and I'd left some lousy weather behind me, too. I was feeling good about having it in my rear view mirror.

In the moment it took to go from asleep to awake, I'd decided to put as positive a spin on this whole Winslow thing as possible. There wasn't any point in ruining any more of my time over it; many of our problems gain even more strength as they weaken us, sucked away as we fret and worry over something we can do nothing about. Yeah, I didn't want the resort to be built. But that was all the due it was going to get from me; a dislike, on par with the one I had for Brussels sprouts. So strong, yes. But not something I'd think about all the time.

I decided to go and visit Luis and talk about the resistance's surrender as part of my continued therapy. I hadn't seen him since the whole thing had began, and he had a way of putting things in perspective that I often relied on during those rare times I was troubled, and he'd become something akin to a wise grandfather for me. And a lot wiser than my own, not so grand grandfathers had been, that was for sure.

I found him as always in his garden. He was tending to his Heliconias, brilliant red and yellow flowers whose buds grew in little opposing spikes, almost like a serrated dagger. We sat down under the shade of his umbrella, and sipped on some papaya iced tea while we talked.

"I suppose you are here because you are having another crisis, Jack," said Luis.

"What makes you say that?" I said.

"Because there is a big hotel coming to di island, and you handle change about as well as you handle women," said Luis.

"You're right on both counts, more or less," I said. "This time the two are even related, although I think I've come to terms with the hotel. But I may have messed up another good thing with someone."

"Jack, Jack, Jack," said Luis. "With you, the two are almost always related. You wanted change so you left Brittany behind, and Isabella wanted change so she left you behind. And what was it with this new girl, Kaitlyn, I'd heard about?"

"I didn't want the coming change and told her so; but this time, that change didn't have anything to do with Kaitlyn, really. I just blamed her for it," I said.

"I see," said Luis. "And about this change, this hotel; I know you. You may have convinced yourself that you are okay with it, but we both know this is not true. Otherwise you would not be sitting here now so I can council you about it."

"Maybe I just came to see my old friend," I argued.

"Si, but you also came because you also needed to," said Luis, and he closed his eyes for a moment. I thought for a second he'd gone to sleep, but he opened them again and continued. "One of the things you still have not come to accept is that nothing stays the same. Do you really think you can make the changes you want in *your* life whenever you want to, and then expect the rest of the world to stay the same just for you, Jack?" said Luis. "It does not work that way. Everyone is like you, hoping to make their lives better. Sometimes that fits in with what we want, and sometimes it does not."

"I know; that's why I've accepted it and moved on. Or at least I had until you told me I hadn't," I said. "Has it ever occurred to you that the reason I don't get over things more quickly is because you tell me I'm not over them, and I keep listening to you because I respect your opinion? I was perfectly content with the whole situation until a few moments ago."

"No, you were not," said Luis, coughing a little. "You may think you were, but..."

"If you say so," I said. There was no point in starting an argument. The last time I'd won one was before I'd left the mainland, and it seemed I was hopelessly outmatched on di island. Instead I looked at Luis; his eyes were closed again, and I figured I should just stop bothering him and let him get some rest. I stood up, and said, "I should go, and work some more on accepting not accepting things; is there anything you need before I leave?"

Luis spoke, his eyes still shut. "Just one thing, and one thing only; please say that you are truly happy."

"Look, I-" I began, or gasped, in exasperation. "Yes, I am! How many times do I have to tell you?"

"Me? None," said Luis quietly. "But yourself, at least once more, so you remember it again. Trust me."

I sighed. "Okay, fine; let me try."

I closed my own eyes, and thought long and hard on the subject. It seemed silly at first, but then I realized I'd forgotten how happy I really was, and how blessed I felt, with or without this hotel business. There is almost nothing we humans don't eventually start taking for granted; the beauty we see in the world around us every day, our family and friends, and even our own happiness. To take the time to savor and taste that happiness like a good meal is to truly know and appreciate it. And when I did so, a soothing wave of contentedness washed over me like the gentle caress of Mother Ocean.

I opened my eyes again. "Yes, Luis. I can honestly say it; I am truly happy," I said, and meant it.

Luis sat there in his wicker chair, eyes closed, looking serene and peaceful in his garden.

I smiled at him, turned, and started to walk away, then stopped. I studied him more closely, and said tentatively, "Luis?"

My old friend didn't answer. And just like that, he sailed away to that one particular harbor.

Chapter 15
"Hey Mr. Marty, time to go home."

It was days later that I finally took the time to talk to Marty. I'd wanted to sooner, but Luis' passing had sent me into a new world of emotions to deal with I didn't know I had. I'd never lost anyone who meant so much to me before; my grandparents and I had never been close, and my own parents were alive and well. I'd been lucky with everyone else in my life; up until now, that is.

It took me a while to come to the realization of the beauty of it all. He'd lived and enjoyed his life all the way from the beginning to its natural end, and that was a special gift. And I think he knew how precious it was, to have the chance to take all his spins in the grand dance.

Maybe some of our lives aren't what we expected, and we may even feel we've wasted them. But that can never be true if we understand that accepting who we are and what we've done with our time is all that matters. Life isn't a test to be passed; there are no grades, and we can't fail at it. We all move on, and we all end the same, and the greatest thing we can accomplish, far more than any riches or fame, is embracing who we are and have been before it's too late.

I knew Luis had done that, which was why I eventually felt so content about his leaving. Yes, I wept, but all good things come to an end, and what matters is having enjoyed them while they were happening. I would miss my old friend, but I was glad for my time with him and the happiness he'd had during his time on Mother Earth.

Marty was another matter, and a difficult one to approach. It was hard to convince myself that I had any right to tell him what to do, when I'd been told by so many people that my own path had been one of utter irresponsibility. Not that I cared so much what anyone thought, and I even enjoyed hearing it, but it did make me wonder if I should be the one handing out advice to someone else on how not to live their life.

But I felt I should at least try for the sake of his family, and because I felt the tiniest bit responsible for his current island state of mind. So I went up to the plantation to talk to him; I was still living in my hut, since I hadn't seen hide nor hair of clipboard and headset, or any other corporate lackeys, for some time now. I had no idea why I hadn't been evicted yet, but it would take me all of about fifteen minutes to move out of my shack when I was finally told I had to, and I wasn't about to surrender the fort until the last possible second. Besides which, the plantation only had one bedroom, which meant I'd have to move Marty out one way or the other before I came inland, and it was probably time to do at least that.

We sat out on the front porch where I'd first met Rodrigo, a bucket of Kaliks on the side table between us. I took a long drink on my frosty, open one, and spit it out; not the delicious beer, but my thoughts.

"Marty, what are you still doing here?" I said.

"What do you mean?" said Marty.

"I mean, why haven't you gone home? This is crazy; you've got a wife and kids back in the states," I said.

"You think I don't know that?" said Marty.

"I have to assume not, since you're still here; at least with a case of amnesia you'd have some kind of an excuse. Or are you trying for a spot on Dr. Phil?" I said. "Have you even called Bonnie, lately?"

"Yes, I have. But what does it matter? We're not getting along, and that's not improving," said Marty.

"How could it? She's not liable to lavish you with long distance kisses while you're sitting here in the sun thousands of miles from home," I said.

"Maybe. But why are you getting on my case all of a sudden, anyway? I'm not doing anything different than you did," said Marty.

"No, you're not. But you are doing it to more people than I did," I said. "And Brittany doesn't count; she'd abandoned me long before I abandoned her."

"Are you trying to tell me you think I should go home? Beg for my job back at Image Makers? Again?" said Marty. "Be miserable for the rest of my life?"

"Yes to the first, no to the second, and not if you can help it to the third," I said. "You know, there is some middle ground between living in hell and giving up on everything in your life, including the good things. Do you really want to abandon your kids, for example?"

Marty sighed. "Of course not. But I didn't know what else to do. I felt trapped, and I was making everyone as unhappy as I was. And I thought maybe just going far, far away might be for the best; they'd get over me eventually."

"I doubt that," I said.

"Well, what do you think I should do, then?" said Marty.

"I told you; go home," I said.

"That's it?" said Marty.

"For now, yeah," I said. "You've got to start there. Sit down and talk to Bonnie. Figure out what you want to do with the rest of your lives, even if it's not together. Settle everything first; if you still want to come here afterwards, after you're damned sure it's right and you've explained it all to your family, then go ahead and do it. But not like this. Otherwise, you're just going to end up with regrets, and that'll screw up even a life on di island, and one of those doesn't deserve that kind of treatment."

"Anything else?" said Marty.

"Nope. Either work things out or wrap things up; no lose ends. Even I gave my plasma TV a good home before I ran away," I said. "Although maybe you weren't such a good foster dad after all; you abandoned it back there too, you know."

Marty pondered my words a moment. "So you're saying it's not so much what I've done, but how I've done it?"

"That part's for you to decide," I said. "The thing is, I don't know if anyone can know what someone else should do in life, especially when it comes to something this heavy. Hell, I don't even like telling someone what they should have for lunch. But I do think when it affects other people that everyone should take the time to think it through and be damned sure they know what they're doing before they do it. And I'm not sure you did that...did you?"

"No, I didn't," said Marty. "But that was sort of the point. The whole *"I'm gonna live my life like a Jimmy Buffett song"* deal, remember? Leap before you look?"

"Yeah, I remember," I said. "And I'm still doing it, but-"

"But you were alone," said Marty.

"Aye, laddie," I said.

Marty slumped his cubicle chiseled shoulders in resignation. "Fine; I'll leave tomorrow, and do what you say. But I'm not making any promises I won't come right back in a week," he said. "And I've got to tell you, this isn't the kind of conversation I expected to have with you."

"I'm sure it isn't. If it makes you feel any better, even I don't know what's going on with me, lately. I'm sending you home, and I put the kibosh on any pirate attacks on the Winslow people when every instinct told me to keep firing with all guns blazing. I'm worried I might be starting to do that thinking stuff again," I said.

"So what are you going to do about that, Jack?" asked Marty.

I looked at my beer, then picked it up. "I'll tell you what I'm going to do; first, I'm going to drink this beer. Second, I'm going to drink those beers, too," I said, pointing at the Kaliks in the bucket.

"Mind if I have one or two?" asked Marty.

"Only if you beat me to them; it's a beer drink beer world, you know, or something like that," I said. "And after we cannibalize all these beers, we're going to go get Captain Black Dog to fire the cannon for a bon voyage party to you and my beach, before I move out tomorrow and get it over with. It's time to get back to the basics of getting out of bed, when I'm good and ready of course, and just enjoying whatever the day throws at me."

"While I get back to doing just the opposite," said Marty.

"I think you can figure something else out," I said, then clinked my bottle with Marty's. "But just in case, we're gonna have us some fun tonight."

Which turned out to be even easier done than said.

Chapter 16
"If di phone does ring, it's me."

There are times when sitting alone in a quiet little corner of the world seems like the closest thing to heaven on Earth you'll ever feel.

This wasn't one of those times.

If this night was in fact anything like heaven, it means there's gonna be a much bigger party going on up there in the clouds than I'm expecting. I'm not much of a prognosticator when it comes to the afterlife, but I'm hell bent, so to speak, on enjoying my time on Earth on the off chance it's all the time I'll ever get, corporeal or not. And tonight was no exception to my rule.

This evening's luau was in fact dancing dangerously close to too much fun, and I seriously hoped I wasn't about to find out there was a fun barrier a hedonistic fighter jock like me couldn't punch through. It would be depressing to learn there was a limit on something like that, but I had to find out one way or the other, for the good of all mankind. At the least I wanted to push the envelope just a little bit farther, so people would know that just when they thought they were getting too happy, they could safely have another laugh or three without crashing and burning. It was tough and dangerous duty, but I was honored to volunteer for it.

I had the feeling that pretty much di whole island had shut down for this get together, and my beach was filled with wall to wall revelers. Even the most interesting innkeeper in the world was there, as was as Henri. Although it wasn't the first time the Innkeeper had shown up; he liked to bring over his push cart, laden with libations, and run a portable version of the Monkey at my tiki bar, whenever he thought he could make more money there than keeping his own place open.

But Henri had never come to one of my parties, at least before his business's normal closing hour at eleven o'clock. It was good to see him outside of work early for a change, and the best part was (for the rest of us, anyway), he was still wearing his chef's hat.

"You know, you really didn't have to do this, Henri," I said, watching him a sweatin' and a frettin' over the big pot of seafood gumbo that hung over the fire. "That's a whole lot of fine cuisine you're giving away."

"Ya, but da way I see it, it's advertising," said Henri. "I've been tryin' to get more people to come in to my restaurant. Boyd came by and told me you had half di island over here, and now I think the rest come, too. And I figure dis way, I get everyone to try my gumbo at once, and maybe den dey all get hooked."

I leaned over the pot and took a big sniff, making my taste buds start screaming for something more tangible. "Well, if they *don't* get addicted, they need to see a palette therapist, and soon," I said. "Never mind playing for your gumbo, I'd even work for it. Maybe. Not too hard, of course. But if I was going to work for anything at all..."

"Hey, great party, rum dude!" said Luke, an American from Arizona who Marty and I had met when we popped over to the factory to reload my rum supply. He and his friends had come over from Tortola for the day on Roger's shuttle, but had decided to stay the night when they'd heard about my luau. "This is a great island, man!"

"It is, isn't it?" I agreed.

"Yeah; we're gonna tell all our friends about it," said Luke. "Pretty soon, you're gonna have lots of visitors!"

"You don't know the half of it," I said.

"Boss, you're needed on di dance floor, now," said Faith, as she grabbed me by the arm and started dragging me across the sand and away from Luke, before I could decide whether or not to complain about the Winslow to him.

"You and me dancing together, Faith? Whatever will Ernesto think?" I said.

"He'll think I like to dance and he doesn't, like always," said Faith. It was true; Ernesto was one of the few islanders I'd never seen cutting a patch of sand. Faith, on the other hand, had di rhythm of di islands embedded deep in her DNA, and every inch of her brown body could move in whatever pleasing direction she liked. Which often gave me thoughts I shouldn't be having about a friend's wife, but did anyway because I was male. And because Faith was Faith.

But Faith was also faithful, and even though my mind wandered a bit as usual as we danced, I knew that's all that would ever happen. And I was glad (the thinking parts of my anatomy, anyway). Because while I liked Faith and I liked Ernesto, I liked Faith *and* Ernesto, together, even more. They were great people, and despite being total opposites, they were even better as a couple. Which was how all married people should be; better hitched than if they were single, or what was the point?

The music we danced to was being provided by *The Rum Powered Goats*, as always. The Goats were a one to four and a half piece band, depending on who happened to be sitting in at the time. Tonight they consisted of Cavin on guitar, Boyd on the bongos, Michel on the fiddle, and Jedidiah on the steel drum.

Jed had casually picked up his newest creative skill over the last few months, as if it were no big deal as usual. Me, I still struggled with my old guitar, due to a very consistent lack of practice. Which was why I made up the one half part of the band, *when* I decided to join in and ruin a song or two.

Don't get me wrong; I love music more than almost anything else in the world. I can barely do without it for any length of time, and there are those moments I simply have to have it if I'm going to truly enjoy myself. When the boat drinks start sailing for example, music becomes another oxygen; I feel like I'm suffocating if there are no notes and chords floating in the air around me. But I don't need to be the one bartending to enjoy my drink, or the one cooking to savor my food. And music tasted a whole lot fresher without my sour tones smogging it up.

When we'd finished our dance and my harmless fantasizing, Faith guided me over to a seat at the tiki bar. She got us a couple of Mangled Macaws, yet another new concoction the Innkeeper was trying out, this one with pomegranate juice, and said, "We need to talk, boss."

"What did I do now?" I asked, trying out the drink. It was good; scary good, actually. As if the Innkeeper needed yet another enticing, colorful bird for his drink aviary.

"It's not what you did, it's what you didn't do," said Faith. "At least dat's what Marty said."

"Which is what?" I asked, reminding myself to firmly kick Marty in the ass the next time it presented itself.

"You haven't called Kaitlyn since she left, have you?" said Faith.

"Marty told you that, did he? He's one to talk," I said.

"Well, have you?" insisted Faith.

"No, but I'm still trying to decide if I should or not," I said. Which was true; while I certainly wasn't angry at her, Kaitlyn was there and I was here. "I'm not sure I see any point in trying to fix a car that's parked where I can't drive it."

"Boss, what di hell does dat mean?" asked Faith.

"I have no idea. It was the best analogy I could come up with, given all these different winged critters I've been flying with," I said, holding up my drink.

"How about just saying what you mean for a change?" said Faith. "Like, do you love her?"

"Whoa; we're getting a little bit carried away, aren't we?" I said.

"Not really; you either do or you don't," said Faith. "It's as simple as dat, and not nearly so complicated as people make it."

"I suppose you're right, but I haven't really thought about it. We just got along way too well, too easily," I said. "It was very nice; that much I can say. And yeah, I suppose I wouldn't have minded more of it."

"Den call her, and see if you can get some more," said Faith.

"I don't have a phone," I said, using my favorite excuse.

"We'll find you one," said Faith.

"Then I'll call her when you do," I said.

"Promise?" said Faith.

"Promise," I said stupidly, even though I should have known what would come next.

"Good," said Faith. "Ernesto!" she shouted, then turned his way and put her fingers up to her ear in the international phone sign. Ernesto reached into his shirt pocket, and tossed her a cell phone. "Here you go," said Faith.

"Now isn't really a good time," I said.

"Yes, it is," said Faith. "You shouldn't be alone, boss, and now's as good a time as any to do something about it."

"I don't have the number," I said.

"Marty said her number is di twelfth one down," said Faith. "It's his phone, and he saved it di last time you used it, while Kaitlyn was still here."

"You thought of everything, didn't you?" I said.

"Marty and I, yes; dis was his idea, but I was glad to help," said Faith.

"He's a sneakier bastard than I give him credit for," I said, looking over at him. It was hard to imagine such a devious brain lurking in his noggin; he looked so innocent, dancing around with the hollowed out watermelon on his head.

"He said to tell you you needed to take your own advice," said Faith.

"I knew I should have kept my big mouth shut and left him alone; that's what I get for meddling," I said. "But maybe he's right. Give me the phone."

I took the cell from Faith, and got up and walked over to a relatively quiet area, which meant about a five minute stroll down the beach to get away from the noisy festivities. Finally I found a spot I liked, and scrolling through the contacts on the phone, found Kaitlyn and dialed.

I didn't really expect her to answer, and I was sort of hoping she wouldn't. Then I could just leave a message and get off easy, and hope she would call me back. Of course Marty's phone would be god knows where by then, but I wasn't thinking too clearly at the moment.

As the nearby ocean lapped against the sand to the rhythm of the phone beeps, I waited and wondered what I was going to say. I took the moments to remember what is was like to just sit with Kaitlyn by that ocean, and how she had managed to make such an already wonderful thing feel even better. I realized I missed her, and perhaps because of how easily we'd come together, had taken that feeling of being with her for granted. And by the time she answered, It became pretty obvious what I wanted and needed to say.

"I'm sorry."

Chapter 16
"Sendin' my old friend home."

I woke to the sound of pounding in my head; it reminded me of a morning way back at the Ramada Inn in Minnesota, and just like then, I realized the noise was coming from outside sources and not my noggin.

There was someone at my door, to be precise. I hoped for a fleeting moment that it might be Kaitlyn, but doubted she'd changed her plans that quickly and had shown up now instead of in the month we'd talked about last night. But hey, ya never know.

I got up and padded to the door and opened it, and stared blearily at the two figures outside. If I'd propped my lids open farther I might have been able to see them better, but it wasn't often I didn't get to follow my sleep session through to the end, and I wasn't happy about this one being cut short. So whoever the offending visitors were, they were only getting my bare minimum necessary to walk eyeballs.

"What," I said, using the shortest greeting I could find as well (I would have used *yes,* but it seemed too polite).

"Ah; Mr. Danielson," said clipboard.

I groaned, something I was out of practice at, but found was like riding a bicycle. "What the hell do you two want? Wait, let me guess; it's moving day, isn't it? Look, I was planning on doing it today anyway; just give me an hour to find my consciousness, and I'll be gone. I know it's around here somewhere..."

"We are here about just that, but we need to talk," said headset.

"Now why would I want to do that?" I said.

"Because we've hit a bit of a snag, and thought that maybe you could help us," said clipboard.

"The snakes in your beds didn't convince you otherwise?" I said. "I'll have to order out for some pythons next time."

"Yes, well, we know you've had something to do with a few...incidents," said clipboard. "But we're willing to forget all that. Can you come out so we can chat?"

"Fine, give me a minute," I said, and started to close the door. I opened it again, and said, "On second thought, not here; I'm starving. Why don't we meet at Robichaux's and, what does your species call it again? *Do lunch?* Let's say at...what time is it, anyway?"

"Ten o'clock," said headset, looking at his watch.

"Okay, in an hour, at eleven," I said.

"Fine," said headset, and they started to walk away.

I went to close the door and failed once again, and said, "Cancel that memo; better make it noon. I've got something I need to do, first," then slammed the door shut once and for all.

An hour later, I stood on the dock next to Gus' old seaplane, Marty by my side. He didn't seem all that happy to be leaving, so I tried to make him feel better.

"You're doing the right thing," I said.

"I know," said Marty, sullenly. "But I still feel like I'm being grounded and sent to my room."

"It'll be good to see your family again though, won't it?" I said.

"Yeah, but I just don't know what I'm going to say to them," said Marty. "I talked to Bonnie on the phone and told her I was coming, and at least she was civil, and all things considered I guess I give her credit for that. But how we're going to work things out so everyone's happy, I have no idea."

"You'll do it. You weren't going to be happy for long hiding out here on di island, either," I said.

"If you say so," said Marty. "I would have been willing to give it a try."

"It's time to go," said Gus, having finished all his pre-flight checks.

Marty looked even more depressed, and I couldn't take it any more. "Look, if you don't want to go, then don't, especially if you're just doing it because of me," I said.

"You mean it?" said Marty.

"Of course I mean it. It's not my island; I can't make you leave. And it's not going to do any good anyway, if you're not serious about it," I said.

"Thanks for saying that," said Marty.

"So you're staying, then?" I said.

"No, I'm going," said Marty. "I have to, and I want to."

"Then why are you being so mopey about it?" I asked.

"I'm not; I'm just hungover from your damned luau last night," said Marty, rubbing his forehead. "And if there's one thing I'm not looking forward to right now, it's getting in this little plane."

"But I thought...never mind," I said. "You could wait and take Roger's shuttle."

"That didn't work out so hot on the way here, either," said Marty. "Remember? But at least I'm used to flying, so I guess it's off I go into the wild, turbulent, yonder with this madman."

Gus smiled evilly, and climbed into the cockpit. Marty and I shook hands, and he joined him inside.

"Hey, if nothing else bring the whole family here for a visit," I said through the open side window. "You can stay at the new resort."

"We won't be able to afford it; the place is gonna be well out of our price range," said Marty. He waved, and I stepped away and down the dock as Gus fired up the engine. I watched as they taxied out to sea, where Gus opened up the throttle, and the yellow plane soon lifted off the green waters into the blue sky.

I waited until they soared out of sight, my solemn mission accomplished, then headed towards Robichaux's for my power lunch.

Chapter 17
"I am di person Anderton warned you about."

I arrived at Robichaux's and found the terrible two seated at a table on the deck. I sat down and joined them, and after we'd ordered (I had the Andouille sausage with a cup of conch chowder) got down to business.

"So how can I help you guys?" I asked. "Or should I say, how are you deluded enough into thinking I can help you guys?"

"It has to do with the land your beach house sits on," said clipboard.

"Beach shack; or hut. Call it what it is," I said.

"Fine; your beach hut," said clipboard. "It would seem there was a bit of a snafu when the sale of the land was drawn up."

"What exactly does that mean?" I asked, sipping on my Cajun spiced Bloody Mary, and looking out at the ocean where a large, beautiful, sailing yacht I'd never seen before sat anchored.

"It means, Wonbago ripped us off," said headset. Clipboard looked at him, and he said, "Well, it's true, and there's no point in beating around the bush about it."

"That Wonbago's a wily one, but I don't know what that has to do with me," I said.

"When he drew up the property lines in the sales contract, he left out the plot of land where your beach hut sits," said clipboard. "*Exactly, just* the land where your beach hut sits. Meaning, you still own that."

"I do?" I said, most interested in this new development. "I was wondering why you guys haven't made me move out yet."

"We've been arguing back and forth with him for a couple of weeks now, ever since we discovered it," said clipboard.

"And knowing him, I'm guessing that hasn't been too fruitful," I said with a happy smile. "How did you guys miss that during the sale, anyway?"

"We evidently didn't look at it closely enough," said headset.

"Or, you thought he was a simple islander and underestimated him," I said. "Right?"

"Yes," said the two of them together, irritably.

"That was your first mistake," I said. "So what now? Is Anderton going to cancel the resort?"

"We can't; not the sale of the land, anyway. We already own that, so we'd prefer to go forward with the hotel," said headset. "But we'd like to buy your plot from you; we'll give you a very good price."

"I bet you will," I said. I was feeling positively giddy with my sudden bargaining position; it was nice having them over my rum barrel. "What if I'm not willing to give it up? Would you just build around me? It might be nice to have a dolphin shaped pool on my doorstep."

"If you wouldn't budge, we'd have to cut the land up and try and sell it off to someone else; we can't build with you there, smack in the middle," said clipboard. "But that wouldn't be our first choice; it could take years to find a buyer."

"Well, whatever shall we do?" I said.

"I told you he wouldn't cooperate," said clipboard. "Anyone who would put a live lobster in our toilet isn't going to be on our side."

"Somebody did that?" I said. Headset nodded. "Well, it wasn't me; not that I don't approve, mind you. I just wonder who it was..."

"I don't know, but it was a close call, and it was enough to make us borrow the Anderton III to stay on, out there where it's safe," said clipboard, indicating the sailing yacht I'd been admiring.

"That's yours, huh? Nice corporate perk," I said.

"Thank you," said headset. "So are you dead set against selling to us, or do you want to at least hear our offer?"

"Give me a second to think," I said.

It seemed I'd suddenly been handed all the power I'd wanted to stop the Winslow from ever being built, or at least delaying it and any other such resort for some time. But I'd made a decision to do what I thought was best for everyone on di island, and not just for myself, and I wasn't going to back out on it now; I'd be liable to have a visit from the ghost of Luis past some night soon. But that didn't mean I wasn't allowed to try and make that decision a happier, and hopefully better one.

"How about you two listen to my offer instead," I said.

"Alright," said clipboard, obviously bracing himself for the worst.

"Can we all agree that if I don't give up my land, Anderton stands to lose a lot of money?" I said.

"Possibly," said clipboard.

"Come on; you can do better than that," I said.

"Okay, *probably*," said clipboard.

"That's better," I said. "And I doubt if your bosses will be real pleased with that. But I'm willing to give you an alternative. So here's the deal; I did some research on Anderton. Well, actually, my friend Marty did; it sounded like too much work to me. But you build all kinds of hotels and resorts, not just thousand dollar a night luxury jobs. Am I right?"

"Yes, Anderton's properties *are* diversified," said headset.

"Then this is what I want; I want you to agree, in writing, to put something else on that land. A resort where normal people who don't carry their portfolios with them can afford to come and visit di island. That's the first thing I want in exchange for my land," I said.

"You're kidding, right?" said headset.

"Do I look like I'm kidding?" I said, trying my best to appear serious, which wasn't easy given how much fun I was having.

"We can't just change our plans on the fly," said clipboard.

"Why not?" I said. "You obviously already think di island would be a great place for a hotel; all you need to do is build a less expensive version, one that other Buffett, Warren, would think is beneath him. And you have a piece of land that's not doing anything better at the moment; a piece of land, by the way, with a certain beach shack smack in the middle of it. A shack that's not going anywhere if you don't agree to my demands." I liked having demands; I'd never had any before, and it turned out they were kind of fun.

"What difference does it make to you what kind of resort we build?" asked headset.

"All the difference in the world," I said. "Everyone should be able to come and visit di island, not just rich people."

"If you say so," said headset, scratching his head. "What do you think?" he asked his partner. "Would they go for it back at headquarters?"

"Maybe," said clipboard. "At least we wouldn't be losing money that way. Depending on how much cash he'd want for his final plot."

The two turned and looked at me expectantly. "Well? How much money do you want?" asked headset.

I had the feeling I could pick up some easy dineros, which was very tempting, but something else occurred to me I wanted more instead.

"I don't want any money," I said. "But..."

"But?" said headset.

"I want that boat," I said, pointing at the yacht.

The two turned to look at the large sailboat, then back at me.

"Are you nuts? Do you have any idea how much that thing is worth?" said clipboard. "We'd rather give you a pile of cash than sign that over to you."

"You misunderstand me; I don't want to own it. Well, I wouldn't mind it, but that's not what I'm asking. I want to use it. For say, a week or so?" I said.

"That's it? You just want to borrow our boat?" said clipboard.

"Yes; I have a sudden urge to take some of my friends on a little cruise," I said.

"That maybe we could do," said headset. "As long as our professional sailing crew manned it; we do that all the time for VIPs."

And now all of a sudden, I was a VIP. "Even better; personally, I just want to enjoy myself. I'm not much on climbing rigging or swabbing decks," I said.

Just then Boyd brought over a tray with our food; he was sunlighting as a waiter at Robichaux's today, and as he set out the plates in front of us, clipboard said, "Do we have an agreement, then? *If* corporate agrees to altering the resort?"

"If yes, then yes," I said. "But I want it in writing, like I said; I don't trust you land pirates."

"You'll get it," said headset. "I think we can talk them into it, given the fact they don't have much choice."

I picked up my Bloody, saluted the deal, and took a drink. It was my first power lunch, and I think if Donald would have been there he would have tried to hire me as his apprentice on the spot. But hopefully my corporate days were over as quickly as they'd begun.

Though I had to admit, my conch chowder had never tasted sweeter.

Chapter 18
"He went to Venezuela."

Two weeks later, my new business partners still hadn't gotten back to me; in the meantime, I'd spent the days confidently putting together a pirate crew for our great sailing adventure, convinced it was going to happen. In the end, I decided to make it a no wenches trip; boring, I know, but my pirate lore told me that having a woman on board was dreadfully bad luck. And I wasn't into sinking, being cursed, coming under attack by zombie pirates, and/or being eaten by sharks. Death by mermaids maybe, but I doubted I'd get to pick my demise, so Faith and the other gals would have to stay home.

After much negotiations and debating about who could give up their responsibilities for a solid week, the following scallywags finally signed on board; Jolly Roger, Gus, and Crazy Chester. I was surprised and a little disappointed they were the only ones I was able to talk into it; we did have room on board for a few more, and I'd been imagining a much bigger boat party.

But Ernesto had a sugar cane harvest coming up, and I don't think he wanted to be away from Faith for that long. Cavin was anxious to get started on a new rum we'd been discussing, and I got the feeling he wasn't big on leaving Faith for any length of time either, for different reasons, since she kept threatening to undo the changes he'd made around the factory since officially taking over from Luis.

Boyd had mumbled something about a statute of limitations having not yet expired regarding a stop I was planning to make in the US, and wouldn't elaborate more. Which was the only reason Roger could even come along, since Boyd agreed to take over his shuttle pilot duty while he was away. Jedidiah had some new top secret project to work on he refused to discuss with me, while Pat, well Pat was just plain scared to death of sailing, and had been ever since he'd first seen Jaws as a kid.

As for the rest of di islanders I'd asked, they'd all seemed to have an excuse of some sort. But I think the simple fact was that most of them were pretty content to stay right were they were, and had no real desire to go tooling around on the ocean in a big fancy boat. They were happy with their day to day lives, which I couldn't blame them for since I certainly was, too. I just felt the need to throw in a little high seas adventure while I suddenly had the chance.

So once I had my final little crew all set, I decided to just be happy with the people that *were* coming with me. They were all good friends; even Gus, who gave me a hard time constantly, but that's what I'd grown to love about him. We four pirates all got along most excellently, and I knew we had the makings of a great and memorable trip.

Which was why I had to ask myself if I was nuts when I suddenly recruited one last buccaneer.

I hadn't planned to; it just slipped out during one of those feel good moments. Uncle Captain Billy Black Dog and I had been sitting and talking on the Rum Runner, his old, grounded smuggling boat. I'd just mentioned the new coconut rum that Cavin wanted to make, when Black Dog spied something over my shoulder, and stood up as if preparing to bolt into the woods, something he did whenever he felt the need to escape. But this time he held fast, and I too got up and turned to see what he was looking at. And there, coming down the beach, was Boyd, with a man I'd never seen before.

Along with Sam.

The man had Sam on a leash, but when the lab started yanking excitedly on it, he leaned down and set him free. Sam bounded down the beach, up the ramp, and onto the familiar boat, where he began to merrily jump up and down on Billy.

As for Billy, I didn't know when I'd seen him look so happy, except perhaps for the day I'd first given Sam to him, and then he'd been a bit pensive. But now he just beamed ear to ear, and it was good to see. My uncle had come a long way since I'd first met him, when he'd wandered di island, well, like the ghost he pretended to be. He spent a lot more time now with people, and though he'd probably always be a pirate, at least he was back in the land of the living. And what was wrong with being a pirate, anyway?

Boyd and the man approached the boat, and Boyd said, "This is Eduardo; he just brought Sam back to us."

"Where was he?" I asked. Billy was busily ignoring everything but Sam's ears.

"He was in Venezuela," said Eduardo.

"What?!" I said.

"Si. Our ship was in port here a few months ago, and I remembered seeing Sam on the docks with a barefoot man with no shirt," said Eduardo.

"Crazy Chester," I said.

"Perhaps; he did look a little crazy," said Eduardo. "Anyway, I remember stopping and petting him, Sam that is, and then going about my work loading and unloading. Eventually we set back out to sea, and about an hour later we discovered Sam; he must have run on board at some point. I wanted to bring him back to shore right away, but our captain didn't want to fall behind just for a dog."

"I see; are you listening to all this, Black Dog?" I said.

"Black dog?" asked Eduardo, looking at the lab.

"No, Black Dog is...never mind," I said. "Captain?"

"Yes; Sam out to sea, captain a blaggard," said Billy, absentmindedly.

"I know how much a dog can mean to someone, even if my captain doesn't; so when we got home to Punto Fijo I took care of Sam until we went back out on the ocean. It took a while, but we just now pulled into port here," said Eduardo.

"Well, it was awfully nice of you to do all that; and Sam certainly does mean a lot to my uncle," I said. "I'd like to give you a reward."

Eduardo held up his hand. "That's not necessary, senor," he said.

"Are you sure? I own Di Island Rum Factory; how about I send a few cases back to your ship with you?" I said.

"Of rum?" said Eduardo. "Si, I think my shipmates might like that!"

"I hope so, or I'm gonna start wondering about modern sailors," I said. "I'll run over to the factory right now and have it brought to the docks; what's the name of your ship?"

"The Isabella," said Eduardo.

"Well, that's plain weird," I thought.

Eduardo reached over the rail and scratched Sam a couple of times, then waved goodbye and headed back towards his ship with Boyd.

"So, Captain Black Dog; you think maybe you owe somebody an apology?" I said.

"You're right," said Billy. "I'm sorry, Sam; I'll never let you out of my sight again, matey."

"Not him!" I said. "How about a two-legged friend?"

"I suppose you mean Captain Crazy?" said Billy.

"Aye," I said.

"Do I have to?" whined Billy. "Being a pirate means never having to say you're sorry."

"Yes, you have to," I said, and that's when the thought occurred to me and came charging out before I could stop it. "In fact, why don't you come on our pirate cruise, and you can do it there."

"Pirate cruise?" said Billy.

"Er, yeah," I said, wondering instantly what the hell I'd done. I loved this crazy old uncle of mine, but taking him on a ship for a week seemed more insane than most of the things he did and said that made me wonder how insane I was to offer to take him along to begin with.

"Can I bring my mate, Sam?" I said.

"Of course," I said. Sam was a good dog, and he was already a world traveler with four seasoned sea legs, so he'd be the least of my worries.

"Then pipe me aboard, lad!" said Billy. "It'll be a pirate's life for us for sure!"

Anderton III, heave to, batten down the hatches, and prepare to be boarded.

Chapter 19
"We gotta get away to where di yacht leaves from."

Word finally arrived that Anderton Hotel Properties had caved in to all of my demands. A more modestly priced resort was to be built, modeled after a successful design they'd done in Barbados. It still wasn't exactly Days Inn pricing, but with a little saving most travelers would be able to afford it without mortgaging their home and emptying little Bobby's college fund. Victory was mine, and I felt pretty good about it. And about the Anderton III moored just off shore and waiting for us to come aboard.

On the down side, I said goodbye to my beach shack, quickly moving all my belongs over to the living room of the plantation the day we were to leave. I didn't know if my hut would still be sitting there when I returned or not; the Anderton generals might take great joy in knocking it down as soon as possible. But in any case, it was mine no longer, and it made me feel far sadder than vacating my fancy condo in Minnesota those years ago. Gracias por todo, my little hacienda.

My fellow pirates and I met down on the docks early the morning of our departure, meaning just before noon. The crew sent the yacht dinghy in to pick we and our luggage up, and before long we found ourselves on the deck of the magnificent ship that was far larger and grander than I'd estimated from shore.

While I would have been happier still with an old clipper ship, something more akin to what real pirates might have sailed the Spanish Main in, it was hard to complain about the Anderton III. Manned by a crew of five, she was a hundred foot plus motorized sailing yacht with every amenity you could wish for, and then some. It was the kind of ship you saw in movies about jet setting foreign leaders, with Jason Bourne stowed away somewhere down in a storage compartment, waiting to pop out, lose his memory, and spawn some sequels.

I managed to call dibs on the biggest cabin, the king stateroom, one of four guest accommodations. Roger and Gus each took their own room too, which meant that Captains Crazy and Black Dog (and Sam) were bunking together in the fourth, which had been my plan ever since my tongue had decided to invite Billy without my permission. I hoped it would bring the two together, and wouldn't instead lead to any duels across the deck.

As I stood with my friends on the upper aft sundeck, waving to the handful of people who'd gathered to see us off, it was hard not to feel like the king of the world. We sailed on blue green waters under a Caribbean sun and sky, a lifetime or two's worth of wages carrying us along. All I could think of was how lucky I was, and how being a slacker doth definitely have its privileges.

When our friends on shore finally faded out of view, I passed out the mango daiquiris to my motley crew that Ramirez, our steward, had prepared for us. It was customary on the ship to begin a cruise with a champagne toast, but I didn't think it fit our style, and had insisted on boat drinks on the boat instead. I raised my glass, and said, "Here's to enjoying the fruits of our plunder; like Jack Sparrow, we snatched victory from the jaws of defeat by getting damned lucky, and now stand on the deck of the enemy's ship, taken a prize, drinking their rum. Long live we happy band of pirates; arrr!"

"Arrr!" agreed me shipmates, and we tipped up our glasses.

"Well said, lad," said Billy, dressed as always in full pirate regalia. I had to give the Anderton's crew credit; they hadn't batted an eye at his appearance, and were undoubtedly professionals well trained in the art of ignoring all sorts of oddities and indiscretions from their passengers. The five Anderton vessels in their fleet were used to take out VIPs staying at their resorts throughout the Caribbean and elsewhere, which meant rock stars, athletes, and politicians had stood right where we were now. So no matter what crazy thing

Billy might do, it was likely to be tame in comparison to the antics of that lot.

"So what's the plan, mon?" asked Roger.

"The plan?" I said.

"Yeah, where are we going?" asked Gus.

"No place," I said, and shrugged.

"No place?" said Chester. "What do you mean?"

"I mean, we're not going anywhere; at least for the first few days. We're just going to sail around and enjoy the ocean, the boat, and each others company," I said.

"Sounds boring," said Gus. "And who said I enjoyed any of you guys' company?"

"Look; we just came from di island," I said. "What would be the point of sailing a few miles, getting off, and going to another island?"

"Women," said Gus.

"Besides that," I said.

"I didn't think there was another point besides women," said Gus.

"You told me you were happy we weren't bringing any wenches along," I said.

"With us from di island, yeah," said Gus. "I know them, and they all know me, and all too well. But right now, we have a hundred foot luxury yacht in our pickup arsenal to use on women that *don't* know me, and I don't think we should waste it. Oh, but, I forgot; you're in love again, and Kaitlyn's not here, so none of us get girls."

"That has nothing to do with it," I said. "And even if it did, it's my boat, so it's my plan. If you don't like it, you should jump off now while di island is still in sight. I don't think the sharks would eat you; you're probably pretty disgustingly pickled by now."

"Well, what about after those first few days?" asked Roger. *"Den* are we going somewhere? Not dat I mind a few *more* days on the sea."

I'd forgotten that sailing on the blue was basically Roger's job, so I didn't know how excited about more of it he'd be, but a plan was a plan. "Then we go to Key West for a couple of nights," I said.

"Is it okay if we talk to women there, or are we just gonna ride the Conch Train round and around?" said Gus.

"Do whatever you want," I said. "By then, I'll probably be glad if you wander off someplace and disappear."

"So will I," said Gus.

It was just the sort of conversation I was used to having with him; if I'd instead told him we were heading straight to another island where they were shooting the next Sports Illustrated swimsuit issue, he would have complained about that, too. So I'd given up on trying to please him, and just did whatever the hell I wanted.

"Well, I think it's a grand plan," said Captain Black Dog. "Three days on the open sea, and then we pull into a pirate port. What could be better? So stop yer bitchin', Grizwood, or we'll be makin' you walk the plank; Cap'n Jack's in charge on this voyage."

I was somewhat surprised to find myself so easily promoted by Billy; I figured there'd be a power struggle. "Thanks, Black Dog," I said.

"Yer welcome," said Billy. "Just don't screw it up, or they'll be a mutiny faster than you can say *Barbosa*."

Which was more like it.

Chapter 20
"We're pirates in di palace, and we've got it all tonight."

Ship's log, day one:

Our first afternoon passed rather quietly. The lads behaved themselves for the most part, although bosun's mate Grizwood continues to be insubordinate. I may have to cut off his rum rations, but am worried they may be the only thing keeping him as barely civil as he is.

Crazy Chester has already taken it upon himself to learn sailing from the Anderton prisoners who we force to do all the work on board the ship. Today he showed great aptitude for work in the yardarms, and it turns out he can climb any rigging faster than an undead monkey. But being Crazy Chester, he couldn't also help but show his aptitude for falling into the ocean, doing so on two separate occasions (dang it!).

Myself, I showed great aptitude for lying in my deck lounger sipping pina coladas. Jolly Roger, too, seemed quite skilled in this noblest of naval traditions, and also displayed a knack for telling tales of life on the sea (and land), keeping us entertained and laughing for hours.

Captain Black Dog seems to be in his element, strutting about the deck shouting orders. I think he's

made himself my first mate, which I have no problem
with, as long as he continues to be good. Although I
did catch him trying to run up the pirate flag he
routinely flew back on di island. I tried to explain
about modern day pirates and the United States Coast
Guard, and their rather large guns, but I'm not sure he
fully understood. I confiscated the flag, but will have
to keep an eye on him to avoid any run ins with the
Royal British Navy.

As for Sam, he seemed content with trying to
turn multiple levels into poop decks, another situation
I will have to watch closely.

"Land ho!" yelled Gus, again.

"Yes, we know," I said. "It's Puerto Rico. Has
been for about an hour."

"Just wanted to make sure you knew it was still
there," said Gus. "And that they're on friendly terms
with us..."

"Thanks for the info," I said.

"...especially the senoritas," said Gus.

It was early evening on our first day, with
twilight just setting in, and Gus was doing a great
nautical version of *are we there yet?* I'd been enjoying
just floating along, but he was already starting to
weaken my defenses, with a barrage of comments like
I smell coconut oil, I smell perfume, and *I smell*

bikinis, while pointing out every land mass we came anywhere near.

"We're not stopping, so knock it off," I said. "If we did, we'd never make it to Key West with enough time for a two day stay, and I want to see my town again." I turned to Chester. "You know, I never realized how far you travel every time you come to di island from the Keys; no wonder you don't pop over for a visit more often."

"It's a big ocean," said Chester, keeping it short, not wanting to interrupt the rhythm of the crab bites he kept tossing into his mouth.

Ramirez had been waiting on us hand and foot, to an almost embarrassing degree. And with Crazy Chester's appetite, the horsey doverays had been coming out of the galley on a steady basis. I wasn't used to all the attention, and it felt a little weird to me, but obviously Chester (and pretty much everyone else) didn't have a problem with it. I also couldn't help but think that it was kind of ironic that we were being treated as if we were staying at a luxury resort like the one we'd (except for Roger) tried to keep from coming to di island, and it was how we'd ended up on the boat to begin with. Life was a funny little thing, filled with quirks and twists. And mahi-mahi nachos and conch fritters.

Roger came up from below decks, made up a plate of food from Chester's personal buffet, and sat down in a lounger. I realized I hadn't seen him for a while, and asked him about it.

"Where have you been all this time?" I said. "Did you do some fishing like you said you were going to?"

"No, I was down in me room watching *Iron Man* on me big screen," said Roger, smiling.

"You've got a big screen? And movies?" asked Gus.

"Ya, mon," said Roger. "You probably have a huge TV too, hidden in a cabinet. And di DVDs are in di hallway. I was gonna watch di sequel after I have a snack."

"I think I'll join you; beats staring at the water," said Gus, coming over and grabbing a plate. "Lets just pile up on the food and head right down there."

"Sounds good to me," said Roger.

"You guys are just going to go watch a movie?" I said, disappointed.

"Why not?" said Gus. "It's either that or do what we always do, but on a boat." He and Roger headed towards the stairs, and Gus stopped, and said, "Tell Ramirez we'll take our dinner in two hours," then disappeared.

"Can you believe those guys?" I said to Chester. "Here we are on this beautiful ship, sailing across the Caribbean, and they go down into their room to watch TV."

"Yeah," said Chester.

"I mean, don't they know how cool this is? How special? We watch movies all the time on movie night at Monkey Drool's," I said. "So who in their right mind would want to do it here on the boat rather than hang out on deck next to the ocean and under the stars?"

"Yeah," said Chester.

I sat there mildly fuming for a moment, then looked at Chester, who was just sitting there quietly. "You too, huh?" I said.

"Yeah," said Chester.

"Go," I said, resignedly.

"Thanks," said Chester, and he jumped out of his seat and rushed down to catch the final seating for the flick, but not before resupplying his plate.

I got up, and walked over to the railing of the upper deck where I'd spent most of the day. I looked out over the water, then ever more downwards as my eyes followed our wake up to the back of the ship, where I spied my uncle and Sam sitting on the aft deck. I went over and grabbed a couple of conch fritters, then went down the spiral stairs to join them.

"Ahoy, Captain," I said as I approached. Billy didn't like being sneaked up on, so I usually tried to announce myself.

Billy turned, then waved me over and called out to me, "Lad, come have a seat."

I did so, sitting down facing the ocean. I realized the chairs were pulled into the same position as on Black Dog's Rum Runner's aft deck, where Billy loved to sit and look out at the sea. And Sam was in his usual place, sitting on Billy's right side between us, his head nudged up under my uncle's hand.

"Where's the rest of yer crew, lad?" asked Billy.

"They deserted; left me for Robert Downey Jr.," I said.

"Well, ya can't blame them for that, can ye?" asked Billy.

I looked at Billy. "You don't even know who he is," I said, then sighed. "I guess I just thought everyone would be more excited about this cruise."

"Matey, ya gotta realize they all already spend a lot of time traveling around the Caribbean; Roger and Chetster in their boats, and Gus flying over the top in that infernal contraption of his," said Billy. "So it's nothing new to any of them."

"Well, it's new to me," I said. "I've been out riding with all three of them; I've gone fishing with Chester, flying with Gus, and taken Roger's ferry to visit the Soggy Dollar. But this; this is different. It may not feel like like we're explorers or pirates, but I do feel different, as if I'm not attached to any place right now. Which I suppose I'm not, since my real home has probably been knocked down by now."

"That's what a ship is; freedom. As fer yer place, it'll all work out in the end, lad; it always does," said Billy. "It looked like we were going to lose the war, too, and look what happened. A compromise was reached we can all live with, and we got one of East India Trading Company's ships in the bargain."

"I suppose," I said. I closed my eyes and let my other senses take over to help shift my thoughts, then shook myself and opened them again. "Anyway, it doesn't matter. If that's how they want to spend the trip, I guess it's fine by me; I just want them to have a good time. And I'm going to enjoy myself no matter what."

"That's the spirit, lad," said Billy. "Every pirate's different, and a good captain knows that if their crew wants to watch *Iron Man, they* better not try and stop them, unless they want a bloody mutiny on their hands."

"You're absolutely right," I said. "I'll just...wait a minute; how do you know about *Iron Man?*"

Captain Billy Black Dog leaned over to me, winked, and said, "Lad, I may be a wee bit behind the times, but I'm not *that* out of touch."

The rest of the evening passed pleasantly by, much more like the trip I'd envisioned. After the second feature at Roger's cinema ended, we enjoyed a delicious meal of Caribbean Grouper and fettuccine, followed by the five of us sitting out on the aft deck until the wee hours of the night. We laughed and spoke and cussed and joked, and had a glass of rum. Even Gus finally stopped whining, despite the fact that the Dominican Republic and more senoritas eventually came into view on our stern side.

When I finally climbed into my too comfy for words bed, I was wonderfully relaxed. It felt good after the tensions of life on di island (just kidding, but it did feel good), and I fell into a deep sleep, with dreams of being in Mother Ocean's bosom.

Which was a little weird, and would be harder still to explain to someone exactly what I meant, but I can say it was an awfully nice place to spend a few hours.

Chapter 21
"I came back, came back, back to Jamaica."

Ship's log, day two:

After rousing myself from my slumber and cleaning off the evening grime, I went up on deck to find a late continental breakfast and Bloody Mary bar laid out on the upper sun deck. I took advantage of both, and gradually became aware of three things; one, my crew was missing. Two, the ship had stopped. And three, there was an annoying, whining sound in the air that wasn't Gus' voice.

After some investigation, I found that Gus and Roger were down at the aft rail, leaning and pointing at something. I joined them, just in time to see my aged uncle go zipping past in the water, laughing, hooting, and hollering from the back of a red jet ski. Seconds later he was followed by Crazy Chester on a blue one, right before he turned too sharply and flew off, skipping across the waves.

I was a little worried at first that Billy would break his neck, or worse, use the jet ski as a boarding vessel on a small fishing boat that happened by, but I soon relaxed; my uncle seemed to be having the time of his life. We humans love speed for some reason, and the last time that Billy had been in control of anything motorized was likely at least thirty years ago. He was making up for lost time, livin' like a pirate at seventy miles an hour.

I took my turn eventually, and had some fun roaring around with Roger. I suppose it's the closest we ever get to being a porpoise, leaping merrily off the waves and out of the water, albeit a bit noisily. Soon though, it was time to load the vehicles back on board and continue on our voyage.

I could have been miffed at our unauthorized stop and ordered the offenders to kiss the gunner's daughter, but decided that maybe the lads had it right. We weren't in any particular hurry, and though being on the ocean was most excellent, perhaps adding in some variety was the way to go.

So five hours later during our trip on a sailing ship, when we reached Jamaica, I made her stop; and we disembarked in Negril.

"George! George, is that you, mon?"

I couldn't believe it; four years later, and he was still there, standing behind the tiki bar as if I'd never left. Not that I hadn't been hoping to find him there, mind you. But for him to still remember me, too...it was nice. Although it did make me wonder once again what the hell I'd done the last time I heard I was in town to become so memorable.

"Jimarcus! My good friend. It's good to see you again," I said, shaking his hand, warmly. Jimarcus had been my favorite bartender during my visit to Jamaica those few years back, before di island, when I was still attempting to escape from civilization.

"You look good, George; healthy, I mean. You be tanned, mon! You're even starting to look like di Clooney," said Jimarcus.

"Yeah, give me another two hundred years to keep evolving and we'll be twins," I said. "Jimarcus, these are my friends," I said, and introduced my crew, including Captain Billy Black Dog, who had drawn more than a few stares along the beach from the tourists.

"Good to have a *real* pirate at my bar," said Jimarcus, grinning and shaking Billy's hand.

"Thanks, laddie," said Billy. "Would ye have some real rum back there for a real pirate? Me throat is awfully parched."

"Make that five of those," I said, then looked around. "Okay, four; Gus can get his own damned drink," I clarified, since he'd already wandered down near the water where the bikini lounging began, and was talking to a couple of young women while pointing in the general direction of our yacht.

"Coming right up," said Jimarcus.

I gazed around the area, which brought back some fond memories. The tiki bar itself looked more or less the same, especially with Jimarcus standing behind it; Jamaican red, yellow, green, and black, replete with thatching. I could see my hotel a short distance down the beach, where I'd spent little periods of time sleeping and recovering, and one rainy evening sitting on my deck contemplating whatever it was I used to feel the need to contemplate.

Over to the left of the tiki bar and closer to the water was my favorite Negril lounger, or at least it was sitting right where mine had been. It was currently occupied by one of those hairy south European macho men whose Speedo bathing suits were unfortunately smaller than a hanky, and I could tell it would have been much happier and well adjusted with me sitting on it. And growing a few feet away from that lounger, my bush was even still there, the one I'd had to stick my head into the morning after a particularly rough night of relaxing. I'm sure it remembered me, too, and my impromptu, er, fertilizing of it. But most likely, it didn't recall me as fondly as I remembered it.

Nothing at all seemed to have changed since my last visit, and it was good to see that some things stayed the same. Going back to a place we know and love is like looking at a favorite photo; we came back for a reason, and that reason is locked away as a picture in our mind, and we're disappointed at first if it's been altered too much.

I hoped Key West would still be as I recalled her, too, when we arrived some time tomorrow or early the next day. I guess progress has to happen most of the time whether we like it or not, but there are places that should never change, and the Conch Republic was one of them.

We sat down at the bar, and I told Jimarcus everything that had happened to me over the last few years. For some reason, I got choked up when I got to some of the parts about di island. Then again, if there's anything we should be more emotional about than being happy and the reasons we are, be they love, family, friends, or finding ourselves, please let me know. And I'll believe it when I see it.

When I'd finished, Jimarcus said, "You been a busy man, mon. I thought maybe you'd work someting out, but you went overboard."

"Yeah, I did," I said. "That's the best way to put it, too, because I just I fell right in."

"Better you than me for a change," said Chester.

"So what's exciting around here tonight?" said Roger.

"You're looking for excitement?" I said. "I never knew you were the type."

"On di island, maybe not so much. I like di quiet. But here? You know, I be home again, where I grew up," said Roger. "Makes me feel like whooping it up, for some reason."

"Well, there is gonna be a reggae band playing on di stage there when di sun goes down," said Jimarcus.

I looked and found that something had changed, after all; there was now a low, wooden platform where some picnic tables used to be, where I'd sit and add to my journal on my laptop. "So that's a stage, huh?" I said.

"Ya, mon; dey should start settin' up soon," said Jimarcus.

"Cool; I feel like dancing," said Jolly Roger, boogieing a bit in his seat.

"Didn't you say we were gonna head out in a few hours?" said Chester.

"What? You're not gonna leave so soon, are you George?" asked Jimarcus.

I checked out my fellow pirates, to see how difficult it might be to round them up. I knew Roger's vote; he'd made that clear. But Gus was now sitting on the edge of one of the lady's loungers, a bottle of something in his hand, wildly gesturing as he always did when he talked. I found my uncle was sitting on a stool on the other side of the bar in the middle of a group of young men and women, laying on the piratitude, much to their apparent delight. As for Crazy Chester, if there was music to be had, I knew he was always dusting off the dancing shoes he refused to wear.

"Yes, I did say we'd be leaving; no way to make it to Key West tomorrow if we don't," I said. "But I remember a question I used to ask myself while sitting in the Schooner Wharf Bar for hours, in the midst of three hundred and sixty-five other bars; *You're already enjoying yourself, so is there any reason to get up off your ass and go look for fun someplace else?*" And just like then, I don't see one right now, so the Conch Republic will just have to wait for one more day."

"Irie! Di Clooney is back in Jamaica," shouted Jimarcus, then he leaned in close to me. "Does this mean you be buying a round or two like always, George?"

"Light 'em up," I growled.

What the hell; if I was going to act like an actor, I might as well have the bar bill of the rich and famous to go with it.

Chapter 22
"They don't dance like Danielson no more."

Maybe we hadn't managed one love, or one heart, but my friends and I were together, and we were feelin' alright. And so were all our new acquaintances, thanks to the two rounds I'd purchased for anyone who'd been sitting or standing anywhere near the bar at the time.

Of course, when I say two rounds, I mean however the hell many rounds I'd really bought, including all the ones I'd paid for after I'd stopped counting. I'd realized the bill was about to be severely beaten by an ugly stick, and figured if I didn't keep track early on I'd probably be too happy to remember the total when I signed it at the end of the night as well. That way I'd never know just how homely the thing had become, which was good, since the tab was likely to turn into a Medusa.

The reggae band, *Beat Roots*, was almost as intoxicating as the Jamaican rum. I'd dance until I was bathed in perspiration, then take a break, and let the cool ocean breeze dry off my skin. Then it was back out onto the sand to repeat the whole process.

And I wasn't alone; the beach was filled with a sea of people, bobbing up and down like waves under the strings of colored Christmas lights. As to who was dancing with who, that changed by the moment, like an island square dance. One minute I'd be partnered up with a turista cutie, and the next, an island girl. Hell, I eventually even found myself dancing with Gus, which told me it was a good time to take one of my drying breaks.

As I walked away from the dance sand, I happened to notice Chester and my uncle sitting together by the water. I decided to sneak over and see if I could hear what they were saying, and if the two were getting along. I managed to get close enough without being heard to sit with my back to them on a nearby lounger (sand and bare feet have a good stealth rating), and pricked my ears up to listen.

I heard my uncle say something I didn't quite catch, then Chester responded, "I know; I love my bar, and I love taking folks out charter fishing on the Lazy Lizard. Even *if* I don't always like the actual people; damned blabby tourists. They never know when to shut up and just enjoy it."

"And Akiko?" said Billy.

"I love her, too. And she hasn't said she's leaving and going back to di island, but I can tell she misses it," said Chester.

"So what are ye gonna do about it?" asked Billy.

"I don't know; I want her to be happy, but I want me to be happy, too," said Chester.

"It's a tough choice, matey. If I was in your shoes, which would be hard since you don't wear any, I'm not sure what I'd do," said Billy. "On the one hand, a buccaneer's life is a solitary life; I'm already married to the sea. But then again, if I had someone like Akiko, well...old sea dogs like us don't get that lucky very often, do we?"

"No, we don't," agreed Chester. He was silent for a moment, then said, "But selling my bar and moving to di island...that won't be easy."

"Change never is, but even a pirate has to roll with the waves, or be capsized and taken down to Davy Jones' locker," said Billy. "Besides, think of all the fuel you'd save if you weren't runnin' back and forth from the Keys all the time."

"That much is true," said Chester, standing up. "But I'm still gonna have to think about it. Thanks, though, for the talk, Black Dog."

"Anytime, Captain Crazy," said Billy.

Chester walked away, and I was just leaning forward to make my escape, when Billy said, "Did you catch all that, Jack?"

I froze, and felt good and stupid, or more correctly, bad and stupid. "Sorry; I didn't mean to eavesdrop," I said.

"Yes you did," said Billy.

"Okay then, I'm sorry, I didn't meant to mean to eavesdrop," I said.

"That's better; you know, you're becoming more like di islanders every day," said Billy. "Except they're better at casually listening in to people's conversations than you are."

"Give me a break," I said, standing up. "I haven't had as much practice."

"So what are you doin' down here, anyway?" said Billy. "All the lasses are up there."

"I could ask you the same thing," I said. "You had a pretty good crowd going by the bar."

"Got to be a bit much after a while; a pirate needs his personal space. In fact, I'm gonna head back to port in a minute or two, and make sure Sam's kept those East India privateers in line; wouldn't want them retakin' the ship," said Billy. "But ye still didn't answer me question. All those wenches and yer talkin' to me? And don't say it's Kaitlyn, cuz she ain't here. There's nothin' wrong with havin' a lass in more than one port, matey."

"Are you saying I should cheat on her?" I said. "I'm surprised at you, Captain. Where's yer sense of honor?"

"I'm a pirate, not a knight, and I'm sayin' I get the feelin' there's no sort of exclusivity contract between you two yet anyway, now is there?" said Billy, scrunching up an eye at me.

"No, not in so many words, I guess," I said. "But-"

"But nothin'! Live a little, boyo," said Billy. "You ain't getting' any younger, you know."

I didn't need to be reminded of the argument I was having lately with myself and the mirror, whether those were sun bleached or gray hairs congregating at my temples. The answer to which depended on whether I felt like being young or wise that day, with youth usually coming out victorious.

"Anything you say, Black Dog," I said. "In which case, I guess I better get back up to the party."

"Good lad," said Billy. "And I don't expect to see ya 'til morning. Just don't miss the boat."

I left my uncle and headed back to the dance floor, only to be passed by Gus, who was stripping off his clothes and laughing as he ran towards the water.

"Oh, hell; not again," I thought, averting my gaze, until a brunette who looked to be in her early forties also passed by me, while doing the same.

I watched the two for a short moment as they splashed into the water, then shook my head and continued on. I searched but couldn't find Chester anywhere, and Roger had mysteriously vanished earlier somewhere along the night's timeline. I was evidently on my own, and had two choices; either head for the safety of the ship, or uphold the honor of our crew by being the last man standing. Of course, I chose the latter.

But it just wasn't meant to be; another hour of steel drum reggae rhythms and sweating on the dance floor, and I soon found myself horizontal. But that's what happens when you try to behave yourself and be bad at the same time.

I don't know if I and di mystery Jamaican girl I'd suddenly found myself with achieved one love together either, but I do know it felt alright.

All alright.

Chapter 23
"Came along a dolphin, he said, Jack Danielson, hello."

Ship's log, day three:

I woke up at sunrise this morning alone on a blanket in the sand, under an overturned boat on supports. My first thought was to wonder how the hell I'd gotten there, followed quickly by, "Oh yeah," and a smile. And then naturally, Kaitlyn popped into my head, and I got up and headed to port.

As I wandered back along the beach towards our ship, I tried to decide whether or not I was going to have to file my new rum memory under guilty pleasures. I didn't have a whole lot of bottles on that rack, because even though I've had my share of bliss, I haven't done much that I've felt guilty about, especially at the same time. You might say I've been a good boy. Then again, you might say I've been a big wuss.

I hadn't meant for my beach blanket bingo with Bryah to happen this time, either. But when it did, I hadn't exactly tried to stop it. I don't know if Kaitlyn and I have any kind of future, but I do know there've been so many missed opportunities in my life with women from too much thinking, that just this once, when I got another more chance, I went with simply being human, and followed my desire instead. And I had a hard time believing that made me a cheating asshole.

So in the end when I put the memory of my fling in a bottle and stoppered it, I scratched the guilty part off the label, and put it on the pleasure rack to age where I felt it belonged. It wouldn't need much refining to be a treasured part of my collection; it already had the complex characteristics of a great memory, and I knew it would hold its rich flavor for many years to come.

As for the bar bill I never saw but could only imagine, I put that memory in a bottle and threw it overboard; I didn't want to have anything to do with it, even though it certainly hadn't been a cheap one to distill. Maybe someday it'll wash up on the shores of Richard Branson's private island, where he'll open it up and be terribly impressed.

"Hey, Jack! Come down here, quick!"

It was Chester, and for a moment I wondered if he'd fallen in again, but he usually he didn't ask anyone to join him. So I reluctantly got up from the lounger I was steadily recovering in, and went downstairs to the lower aft deck where I found he, Roger, and my uncle, all leaning over the side.

"What's up?" I said, going over to see what all the fuss was about; I thought at first that maybe they were doing group upchuck, but then I saw *them*, and was tempted to fall into the water myself.

Them, or *they,* were a small pod of dolphins swimming off the stern side of the yacht, and coming ever closer. I think I yelped a bit in delight, then raced back up the stairs to get my camera, almost falling back down them and breaking my neck before finally squeezing in against the rail to get a good look.

It's hard sometimes to remember what it was like to be a kid, back when everything was new and wondrous. As we get older and experience more things, life can become sort of a been there, done that, affair, and we end up with less and less that puts the spark of youth back in our existence. But when I saw those dolphins, close enough to be a real part of my strange little world, that's how I felt; like a child again.

They swam right up alongside the boat, easily keeping pace with us, glistening in the sunlight in a way that rivaled the aesthetic value of any bikini clad beach bunny. I don't know if life is as carefree for a dolphin as it looks, or if they're just better at handling stress than we are, but watching them was like gazing at pure joy. I quickly took a couple of photos, then put my camera away to soak it all in, trying to let the experience saturate my brain like a marinade. I wanted to be able to taste all the nuances of the memory when I called it up later; the smell of the ocean, the feel of it on my face as the pod's leaps splashed it in the air, and the playful chirps, clicks, and whistles as the dolphins laughed and sang. And the sight of our better looking, much smarter cousins, mucking about and having a good time without any high-tech inventions to help them along.

Our friends stuck around for a few nautical miles, then waved a flipper and bounded off across the ocean in search of other humans to thrill. I watched them go until they were out of sight, missing them immediately when they finally disappeared over the far horizon.

"Now that was something," I said, thinking I might need to bolster the supports on the rack that held all my fondest remembrances; it was sagging a bit from all the new weight.

"Aye, it was very cool indeed," said Billy, evidently affected enough by the experience to pull out a word from his past to describe it. "It's been a long time since I've seen a dolphin on the open ocean."

"There's a pod that visits me about every two or three days on me shuttle route," said Roger. "But I never get used to it; it's always a thrill."

"Too bad Gus missed it; where is he, anyway?" I said.

"Still sleeping it off," said Chester. "He didn't get back until eight, and said he hadn't slept yet;

seemed pretty damned pleased about it, despite being so damned crabby."

"By the way, where did *you* take off to all of a sudden, Roger?" I said.

"I went...someplace," Roger said with a big smile.

"Seems like there was a lot of *traveling* going on last night," I said.

"And you, Jack?" asked Roger. "Did you go someplace, too?"

I looked behind us, and found Marley's Island in our wake, now almost out of sight. "Yes, I did," I said. "I went to Jamaica, mon. My wallet's down, my head's still spinning around, and I left a little girl in Negril town."

Farewell for another while, Jamaica.

Chapter 24
"There's a Chester goin' crazy on Elizabeth Street."

Ship's log, days four and five:

The last fourty-eight or so hours passed with few notable on board incidents. It seems that we five happy pirates are all also slowly getting older pirates, who are getting slower about recovering from more fun than we deserve. So a couple of days of rest spontaneously created themselves, fueled somewhat by a desire to be fresh for Key West. We just kicked back, ate, slept, fished, and enjoyed the ride, without any complaints from even Gus.

Because of our time in Jamaica, we would only have one full day in the Conch Republic. I'd planned on a longer stay, but at least with our morning arrival it would be enough time to do and see all the important things and places I'd been so looking forward to. Key West is the home that would have still been my home if di island hadn't thrown itself and a rum factory into my path, and I'd missed her more than I had realized.

Also of note in realizations is that you don't want to play poker with Captain Billy Black Dog. I knew from past experiences that Gus considered himself a seasoned card player, and Roger was no slouch. But we all got thoroughly plundered by Billy; I

don't know where he learned his trade, but I suspect
it's an old school thing from his days running ganja
around the Caribbean. When the midnight bell tolled
and I left he and Gus at the table, my uncle had plenty
of walking around money for Key West. And judging
by Gus' grouchier than usual mood the next morning,
Black Dog's hold had likely taken on even more
Grizwood gold after my departure. Which made me all
the happier, of course; I loved hangin' with Gus, but if
it pissed him off, it was bound to make me smile.

As I finish this entry, we are pulling into port in
Old Town at last. And just like my very first visit, I'm
way too excited; I need to slow down and savor what's
to come.

Mahi-mahi and any old rum,
Too many Kaliks and just way too much fun...

It was the first real paved street I'd walked down
in a few years, and if it turned out to be my last, I'd be
finishing my career as a streetwalker on top.

Duval.

Duval Street is like an adult version of Main
Street in the Disney Lands, an entryway into the
pleasures of Key West that fills you with a sense of
anticipation. There've been a lot of things I've
forgotten in my life, but how it feels to just be in Key
West isn't one of them. There's an ambiance that fills

the air, so thick and saturating to the senses that when I'm away, I can always close my eyes, remember, and be instantly transported back once again. Maybe not quite as good as the real thing, but damned close.

My crew and I had been walking for some time, one of the simple pleasures of the island. Although there were always plenty of taxis on hand, I'd rarely used them in the past because you never know what you might miss during your stroll. It could be a street performer, something in a shop window, or just a new old place you'd never noticed before because you'd been distracted by something each time you'd previously passed by. There always seemed to be something new to discover alongside the old and familiar.

"Is this it?" said Chester, as we stood at a red light on the corner, while a man in a booth waved wave runner pamphlets at us.

I squinted my eyes against the morning sun and examined the black and white street sign. "No, this is Angela; one more to go, if I remember right."

"I still think the walk would have been better with Bloody Marys," said Gus.

"The anticipation for them builds more this way," I said, as the traffic cleared enough for us to jaywalk across the street with everyone else.

"I'm not real big on anticipating; I prefer to just skip right to *participating* as soon as possible," said Gus.

"We're almost there," I said. "See? Petronia. We turn right up here."

"Not fond of almost, either," said Gus.

"You'll live," I said. "If not, at least it'll shut you up."

"That's what you think," said Gus.

We walked two blocks away from Duval, spotted our destination on the right hand side, and walked through the gate under the big blue sign with the musical notes; Blue Heaven. And moments later, we were seated at a table in the backyard under the almond tree, a round of Bloody Marys in front of us, our breakfasts ordered.

"Happy now?" I asked Gus.

"Completely," said Gus, sipping on his drink.

"It would be a nice change," I said.

"You won't hear me bitch here, I promise; or at the Soggy Dollar, or at the Monkey. Just everywhere in between," said Gus.

"We should keep dat in mind," said Roger. "Maybe we can split up and meet you at di next stop."

I looked at Billy, who was sitting quietly, gazing off into nowhere. "You okay, Black Dog?" I said.

"Hm?" said Billy. "Oh. Aye; I was just thinkin' how much me old port has changed."

"When was di last time you were here?" asked Roger.

"I'm not sure; I'd have to check me logs. But it's been at least thirty years," said Billy.

"Yeah, I bet it's hard to recognize anything," I said.

"No, I saw a few places I knew on the way here; Sloppy Joe's of course, that sort of thing. And a lot of the buildings *are* still standing. But it all just seems busier, now," said Billy.

A rooster came clucking near our table, and Gus said, "You know, up in the restaurants on the mainland, if a chicken was anywhere to be found except on a plate in front of them, people would throw a hissy fit and walk out. But down here, you look forward to seeing them."

"Beats the heck out of seagulls, anyway," said Chester grumpily, having his reasons.

"Hey, we are in the US, aren't we?" I exclaimed, suddenly.

"Yes, we are," said Roger.

"For some reason it hadn't even occurred to me that I'd be back in America for the first time in years, too," I said. "But it feels weird, like I'm still not quite in the US."

"Key West never seems like America to me, either," said Gus. "It feels more like Puerto Rico or something; foreign, but not as foreign as China or Canada."

"Well, I'd like to make a toast, in any case," I said, picking up my glass.

"Oh, hell!" groaned Gus.

"You said you were done bitching, mon," said Roger.

"That's because Jack's never threatened to make a toast in any of the places I mentioned, until now," said Gus.

I ignored him, and continued on. "To Key West; we've all been here before, and we all have fond memories. Here's to making some new ones..."

"Cheers," said Billy, and we tipped up our glasses.

"Now, was that so bad?" I said.

"No, but if you would have said, "We all have fond memories, and here's to making some new ones *together"* I probably would have had to punch you," said Gus.

"Good thing I left it off at the last second," I said.

"I know; I could tell," said Gus.

Even if that *was* what we were doing.

Breakfast was as delicious as always, and well worth the walk, but we lost Billy and Chester right afterwards. It turns out there are limits to things even in Key West, and going into public places without shoes and a shirt like Chester was attempting was one of them (dressing in full pirate gear like my uncle, was evidently fine). It took some pleading for Chester to even avoid being kicked out of heaven and to get his banana pancakes, and though they eventually served him, it was obvious it was going to be a problem for the rest of the day.

Gus suggested Chester go hang out at the Garden of Eden, the nude bar on the island, where he'd be over instead of under dressed. And Billy even graciously offered to go along and chaperone, and keep a weather eye open for things. But Chester said he had other ideas, and that he'd meet up with us later, although he did ask my uncle to go with him. I felt bad and hoped we wouldn't end up losing the two of them for the day, though I had to admire Chester's sticking to his vows. And at the very least it was good to see that he and Billy were not only getting along, but appeared to have become fast friends.

After our break up, Gus, Roger, and I spent a couple of hours man shopping for tee shirts to, as the *Boat Drunks* put it, tell us where we've been. Then we stopped at Margaritaville for a couple of frozen concoctions to help Gus hang on, before continuing our meander towards the harbor and the traditional fish sandwich lunch amidst the castaway surroundings of BO's Fish Wagon. And finally from there we headed those last couple of blocks past Gary Wyland's ocean mural and along the water, and grew close enough for me to hear that song;

"Key West Florida's my home..."

And at last I was back in my home within that home.

Michael McCloud was up on stage, dressed in his official denim shirt and jeans. A few big and not so big dogs were either lounging around under the tables, shaded from the heat, or sniffing around the gravel and cement for scraps. The tall ships and yachts bobbed gently against the docks nearby, and if my blood pressure could have dropped any lower without putting me into a coma, it would have. All of which meant we had arrived at the center of the universe; the Schooner Wharf Bar.

We grabbed a table with an umbrella in front of the stage and sat down, and soon had two buckets of Kaliks in front of us. I looked around and smiled happily; everything was as if I'd never left, and nothing was out of the ordinary. And it stayed that way right up until the moment that Crazy Chester and my uncle walked in.

They spotted us, made their way over through the crowd, and pulled up a couple of chairs and sat down. When the waitress came over I ordered one more bucket of Bahamian gold to keep up with the increase in demand, and attempted to get back to just being at the Schooner.

I tried listening to Michael, watching the stretched out tarps above us rustle in the wind, and observing the brunette two tables to our left. I even got up and checked out the shirts for sale in the back and purchased one, along with five tie-dyed bottle koozies for my crew. After returning and passing them out, I sat back and sipped my beer, and finally couldn't take it any more.

"I give up!" I said. "I can't concentrate on not concentrating until I know, and since no one else is going to ask..."

"Ask what, mon?" said Roger.

"About that," I said, pointing at Chester's chest. "So what the hell is with the coconut bra, anyway?"

"It's the only thing I could find that went with my grass skirt," said Chester.

"And the grass skirt?" I asked.

"It's the only thing that went with my bra," said Chester.

"So then what exactly is the thinking with all...this?" I said, indicating his ensemble.

"Hey, I'm sitting here, aren't I?" said Chester. "No one has asked me to leave."

"And what about your no shoes, no shirt, forever rule?" I said.

"Well for starters, I'm not wearing a shirt; I'm wearing a bra," said Chester.

I looked down under the table. "And those?" I said.

"I got them off the yacht," said Chester.

"And?" I said.

"They're not shoes, if that's what you mean," said Chester. "They're flippers."

"Dey should come in handy when you decide to fall into di water at Mallory," said Roger, grinning ear to ear.

"I like it," said Gus. "It's sort of a hula-scuba look. And hey, it's Key West; you've got a great chance at meeting that special someone with that getup. Hell, I may even have a go at you later if I get desperate and drunk enough."

"I did it for you guys, so shut it," Chester grumbled. "I figured if Black Dog could walk around in a costume then I could, too, and this way I'm not breaking my rule or theirs. Just remember that Akiko and home are only a little over an hour up the road, so you're lucky I don't just head that way."

"It would take you a while, waddling down A1A in your webbed feet," said Gus.

"Well, we all appreciate all di effort, don't we guys?" said Roger.

Everyone murmured their agreement.

"Thanks, Roger," said Chester.

"No problem," said Roger. "But I have to agree with Gus; you be lookin' damned hot, mon."

Chester sighed. "It's gonna be a long day."

"Yes it is," said Gus. "So what's next?"

"You mean, after we sit here for another hour?" I said. "I was thinking we should sit here for another hour."

"Aren't we gonna hit a few more places?" said Roger.

"Yeah, I didn't get all dressed up for nothing," complained Chester.

"Two more hours, and we'll move on, I promise. But I have to do my Schooner Squatting before I can start Duval Crawling," I said. "This place is always my main reason for being."

"Where are we gonna head to then, laddie?" asked Billy.

"Wherever we end up; that's the only thing to do in Key West," I said. "You make sure you don't miss the important places, and after that, it's like you're women in a mall, stopping whenever you see a pair of shoes you like in the window."

"And one of us is even dressed for it," said Gus.

"Grizwood, did I ever tell you 'bout the time I beat the crap out of this seaplane pilot I knew?" said Chester.

"No, you haven't," said Gus.

"Remind me tomorrow; I'll have the story written by then," said Chester.

"Let me know if you need an editor," I said.

"Or a ghost writer," said Black Dog.

Chapter 26
"She never met a number one pirate."

It was right around midnight, and I wasn't famous yet, although I think my uncle and Chester had come pretty damned close.

Finnegan's Wake, Hog's Breath, Captain Tony's, Sloppy Joe's, Willie T's, Margaritaville, The Green Parrot, The Lazy Gecko, The Rum Barrel; and those were just the places I could remember. And I can tell you that most of them will remember Black Dog and Crazy Chester, too.

Somewhere around the Hog they'd begun to develop an act; Billy would announce our arrival to the bar with a hearty *"Ahoy!"* which Chester would follow with a *"Woo-hoo!"* or two. Then Billy would use his poker winnings to buy a round of shots for the table with the comeliest lasses, and Chester would waddle over with the drinks and introduce he and Black Dog. By the time we stopped our wandering at Irish Kevin's, it seemed like the two of them had met half the women on the island.

"How does it feel to be out sex appealed by your crazy old uncle?" said Gus, watching Billy and Chester in the middle of the crowd of women on the dance floor.

"I don't know; how does it feel to be out sex appealed by a guy in a bra?" I said. I wondered how many times Chester's flippers were being stepped on as he schlapped them noisily around while he boogied up a storm.

"Damned annoying," said Gus. "But I'll tell you this; I'm picking one up the next chance I get. Maybe some training coconuts for starters," he said, then he tipped up his glass of rum and finished it off and stood up. "I'm outta here."

"You goin' back to di boat already, mon?" asked Roger.

"No, I'm going to go walk past the gentleman's club a few times," said Gus. "I probably won't go in because I'm not a gentleman, but it'll make me feel better than sitting here being ignored in favor of Barbosa and Gilligan, there. You want to come, Roger?"

"Naw; I never saw di point in all di looking and not touching," said Roger. "Especially from outside on di sidewalk."

"I think I'm going to stay here, too," I said.

"I don't remember asking you since I already knew the answer, but fine, Jack," said Gus. "I'll see you guys back at the boat."

After he'd left, Roger yawned a big yawn, and I said, "I know how you feel; I'm pretty pooped. I seem to recall when I could do this for hours."

"We have done dis for hours," said Roger.

"Okay, for hours *more,* then," I said, bleary eyed. "I'm not as young as I used to be, and tomorrow I'll be younger less."

"So maybe you have to start pacing yourself a little; no big deal," said Roger.

"I know," I said. "And I've still got some miles left in my engine; I just can't go as far with a single tank before I run out of gas. Speaking of which, I wonder if my uncle is ever going to hit E, because it's about time for my bunk. And I wonder if I dare just leave him here, because I'd hate to break up all the fun he and Chester are having."

"What's di worst ting dat could happen?" said Roger.

"Not sure I want to think about it," I said. "Although I suppose nothing could be as bad as how Billy used to be. When I first saw him sitting in the dark inside Monkey Drool's, acting like a ghost, I never would have dreamed that someday we'd be together here in Key West. And that he'd be shaking his pirate booty on the dance floor in Irish Kevin's, surrounded by a bunch of women."

"What was so wrong about being a pirate ghost?" said Roger.

"Nothing, I know; it was all pretty harmless," I said. "It's just good to see him with people again, so I guess I could care less what he thinks he is as long as he's Black Dog the *friendly* ghost."

"Den I tink we should leave, and let him enjoy himself," said Roger.

"Are you sure?" I said.

"No, but how can we really be sure what will happen until we let it happen? You can never know how people are gonna act, because we are all crazy, not just Billy," said Roger. "And besides, Chester is here to watch out for him."

"That's a real comfort; crazy watching crazy," I said, then stood up. "But you're right; my uncle's an adult, and I've got to trust him and give him the chance to be one again."

"Good man, Jack," said Roger.

"Thanks. But I guarantee I'm not going to get any sleep until he comes back to the boat, so I hope it's worth it," I said, and Roger and I left Irish Kevin's and headed toward the harbor.

Of course, I did sleep, because I was damned tired, but in a lounger on deck near the gangway of the yacht. It wasn't all that comfortable, and when I woke up hours later to the sound of Billy singing a bawdy sea tune as he came aboard, I didn't feel as rested as I might have sleeping in my king sized bed below.

But the glowing look and big smile on my uncle's face, the fact that the sun was coming up, and the lipstick on his pirate collar, told me all I needed to know.

Yes, every toss and turn had been worth it.

More than worth it.

Chapter 27
"I just want to go back to di island."

Ship's log, day six:

The Anderton III pulled out of Key West seaport around one o'clock PM today. We had lunch at the Schooner and one more hour of Michael McCloud before our departure to open seas, giving me the chance for a final farewell to the Conch Republic. I don't know when I'll be back this way again, but hopefully I won't let so much time pass before the next visit to my other beloved island.

I tried to grill Captain Billy Black Dog for some juicy details of his apparent rendezvous, but he refused to tell me anything, saying it wouldn't be honorable. I pointed out that he was a pirate and that honor should have nothing to do with it, but he said he was sticking to the code. He's used that excuse many a time in the past, and I'm beginning to think that the code is simply a bunch of guidelines, written to be interpreted any way a pirate wants. All I knew in the end was that Billy was insufferably pleased with himself, and promised to sit down soon and give me advice on women, despite my protests. Not that I didn't need some good advice, of course. Who didn't?

Perhaps the best news of this day came when Marty called Crazy Chester's phone to talk to me.

After some healthy debating and negotiations on the home front, he and his family would be moving to Naples, Florida, to where Bonnie's parents had retired. Maybe living near your in-laws wasn't what every man dreamed of, but it was the price Marty was willing to pay for a change in lifestyle. At least it was going to be warm and near the ocean, and since he'd be living down in Florida year round now, he could work for me again marketing and distributing di rum in the area without traveling for days away from the fam. And I could even give him some decent benefits now that the company was semi-successful. It looked like everyone would be happy in the end, and I was glad for my friend, and pleased that he'd be living near enough so that I could see him more often.

The only other thing I can think of to note, is how quickly time flies when you're having fun (and rum). We'll already be arriving back at di island late tomorrow afternoon, and releasing our plundered ship back into the hands of the East India Company. It's been an excellent voyage, and I'm glad I thought of it.

Even if it has been raining all bloody day today, and the seas are extremely choppy, and my stomach is beginning to feel like something out of Alien. And as the waves go up and down, and up and down, and up and down, yet again and again and again, I need to stop typing right this second and run to the head...

I was more than ready to be back home.

I was starting to really to miss di island now, and the people who lived on it. This was the first time I'd been away for more than a day in years, and life there had become deeply ingrained in my soul. I could see now that a week was about as long as I'd ever be able to be gone before I started doing serious damage to my psyche.

That may have been one of the best things about this trip, at least for me. Being away let me view di island from a better vantage point, one where I could see her more clearly. If you really want to know how you feel about a place, leave it for a while. If you don't miss it, it probably doesn't mean that much to you. And I definitely knew how I felt about my Caribbean home now.

I could also tell that despite my protests to the contrary, I'd still been slightly irritated with the changes that were now inevitably coming to my quiet, secluded, tropical paradise. And more than that, with the fact that di islanders had wanted them to come, as if they didn't know what was good for them. But now I'd been gone long enough to know one thing, and it rang loud and clear in my pounding and wheezy head, like a tolling ship's bell; I didn't give a damn what happened in the future, di island would always be my home. It was truly where my being lived, and no amount of tourists, paved roads, airports, or (shudder, shudder) even McDonald's would alter my feelings one bit. Di surface of di island might change, but my love for her and what lay at her heart would never waver.

So now I'm sitting here in my cabin, holding my stomach, and looking on the bright side about living at the plantation. It *is* more centrally located for starters, so at least I won't be walking across di entire island every time I need to stop back at my place. And the area around the house is quite large, and should be able to accommodate some good sized parties. Maybe some strings of Christmas lights around the yard, and even over the house itself, would make it more festive. Along with a small strategically planted forest of tiki torches, of course.

The truth is, I know the plantation will never be the same as my hut on the beach. *That* I am going to miss, no matter what I do. But I'll always have my time spent there locked away in my memories, like a very extended vacation; *The Castaway Adventures of Jack Crusoe Danielson, the King of Somewhere Hot.*

And I will still have my friends. I'm wondering if Chester will indeed move to di island, and leave *Crazy Chester's Bar and Boat Stop* in the hands of a new owner. It would be hard, I know, but we all have to do what we have to do to try and make ourselves *and* those around us happy.

If only Adam and Eve had stuck with the papayas and mangoes in their garden, we wouldn't have to try so hard now to live together in paradise.

Chapter 28
"I have found me another home."

Ship's log, day seven:

Di end of our trip is at hand, as in almost within arms reach. I'm sitting up in the bow of the ship, watching di island grow larger as we approach. I'm guessing we'll be close enough to drop anchor very soon now, since I can make out details like the southern docks. I should be standing on terra paradiso within the hour.

I'm very happy to be home again. But I still felt a sharp pang when we sailed past the beach where the new resort will one day sit, and saw that my hut was now gone. It didn't look as if much work had been done in the area, just a few stakes placed here and there for measurements, but Anderton had evidently wasted little time in knocking down my rustic little domicile. It's probably for the best that it was done while I was away, though, to avoid any last ditch remorseful attempts on my part to save it by chaining myself to the tiki bar. Which I just realized is gone now, too.

But it's time to move on, and move off the boat. The crew just dropped anchor, and the call has gone out for us to gather our things and disembark into the dinghy. My short lived naval career is at an end, and it's all ashore that's going ashore.

This is Captain Jack Danielson of the pirate ship Anderton III, signing off.

We stepped off the dock onto land, and stood on di island once more. "Well, we're home," said Chester.

"Aye," said Billy.

"Feels good, mon," said Roger.

"Yes, it does," I said. "And I think we should take a moment and say something to commemorate the end of our voyage, don't you guys?"

My crew looked at one another.

"Nope," said Gus.

"I'm good," said Roger.

"I need to go check my hideout for invaders," said Billy, heading off in one direction.

"And I need to go check on me boat," said Roger, going off in another.

"I better fly to Tortola while there's still light; I've got passengers lined up for tomorrow. It's time to get back to work," said Gus, walking down the shore towards where his plane was tied.

"Yeah, I've gotta get sailing, too; I want to get back to the Keys as soon as I can," said Chester.

"But you just left there!" I said. "Don't you want to rest for a while, maybe leave tomorrow?"

"Not really; Akiko and I have a lot to discuss," said Chester. "Bye," he added, before going back out on the dock to where the Lazy Lizard was moored.

"So much for that," I said, standing deserted by the immigration building. Then I noticed Sam, who was still sitting next to me, and gazing up at me expectantly.

"Don't do me any favors," I said to him.

Sam woofed happily at me, and ran off in the direction Billy had gone.

I picked up my bags, carried them over to Da Fish Gutter building where my Indian motorcycle sat waiting, and put them in the sidecar. Moments later I was rumbling down the dusty road towards Sugar Daddy Plantation (the name of which, during our sail, I'd decided to keep), responding to waves and shouts of *"hello"* and *"welcome back"* as I went.

When I got to the Crossroads I decided instead to go to the factory first; I guess seeing some of di islanders made me want to see more of them. I arrived at the building, and shut the engine off, and went inside.

"Boss!" shouted Faith, before running over and giving me a big hug. "It's good to have you back."

"It's good to *be* back," I said. "Have you and Cavin been playing nicely together, or do I have to go searching for his body?"

204

Faith laughed. "No, your going away was just what we needed. We couldn't talk to you, so we had to come to an understanding."

"Which is?" I asked.

"Dat I was right about everyting," said Faith.

"That doesn't sound much like an understanding to me," I said.

"But it is," said Faith. "We finally sat down and talked; after all di yelling, of course. And he saw dat Luis made great rum without modernizing every little ting, and without making everyone crazy by pushing dem too hard. So he said dat dis be Luis' company, and dat we'd do tings di same way he had. Especially since you didn't care one way or di other."

"Glad I was in the decision there somewhere," I said. But they were right; as long as the rum flowed and continued to be tasty, it didn't matter much how it happened. I just wanted it to be laid back; one nasty little corporate idea could spoil di rum for good.

"Hey, boss," said Cavin, walking up to me. "Good to see you again."

"You, too," I said. "So Faith says everything is a-okay here? You guys don't need me for anything?"

"Not really," said Cavin. "It's all good."

I nodded. "I figured you'd have everything under control," I said. "I guess I might as well head up to the plantation and get settled in, then."

"You know, come to think of it, there is one thing you could do before you go," said Cavin.

"What's that?" I said.

"Just below the patio outside there's a bunch of your stuff; someone must have moved it over from the resort property when they took your hut down," said Cavin.

"*My* stuff?" I said. "I thought I got everything before I left on our voyage."

Cavin shrugged. "Well, you must have missed something; can you go out and see if it's anything you want, or if we should just get rid of it?"

I was perplexed, and could have sworn I didn't leave anything behind. "Yeah, I'll go check it out right now, I guess. You say it's by the patio?"

"Yes, just go out back and look over di wall towards di ocean," said Faith. "You'll see what we mean."

"Okay," I said. I went out the side door and across the stone patio, then peered over the low, rough wall. I didn't see what they meant at first, until I looked farther out and down. And then I saw my stuff.

All four walls and a roof of it.

There sat my old beach hut, right where I hadn't left it. It was as if it had grown legs and wandered northwards along the beach, then plopped itself down in this new location.

I couldn't believe my eyes, which were getting all misty on me anyway, and just stood there gawking at it.

"What do ya tink, boss?" said Faith.

I turned, finding she and Cavin, along with many of the workers, standing there behind me.

"What do I think?" I said. "I think I don't believe it."

"It's no big deal," said Cavin.

"No big deal? It's my hut!" I said. "How did it get here?"

"The day you left, Jedidiah and some of the workers started carefully tearing it down. Then they just carried it up the beach and put it back together just like it was," said Cavin.

"Jedidiah did this?" I said. "So that was his secret project. Who's idea was it, anyway? Was it his?"

"It was kind of everybody's," said Cavin. "We knew you weren't too happy about losing your home on the beach. And di islanders who wanted the resort knew you might have been able to block it if you'd wanted to, and didn't. Everybody just wanted to surprise you."

"Wow," I said, a bit overwhelmed. "That's...just too much." I said.

"So you like it, boss?" said Faith.

"I don't have the words," I said.

"The best part is, the land all the way down to the water is part of the factory, so you own it; no one's gonna move you again if you don't want them to," said Cavin.

"Why didn't I think of this?" I said.

"I don't know; we were all kind of wondering di same ting," said Faith.

I wanted to say something before everyone ran off like my crew had at the end of our sail, but nothing great was coming to mind. "Thank you," I said, finally. "Everyone. It's...amazing."

"You're welcome," said Cavin. "Enjoy."

My employees, or should I say, my best friends in the world, headed back into work, and I headed down towards the mirage on the beach. When I got there, I reached out and touched the post on my front porch and found it was indeed real; along with my tiki bar, which had also found its way to this new particular harbor. Aside from a few new rocks and trees, and a stone grill that had manifested during the move, I could have been standing back down the beach on my confiscated land.

I guess the more things changed, the more they stayed the same.

It was good to have friends.

Chapter 29
"Jack and Kaitlyn tryin' to get together again."

I spent the rest of my first day back on di island getting situated in my new old hut. Not exactly a time consuming project, since I lived like someone, well, living in a thatched hut on the beach. But getting situated also meant taking a couple of naps, and making sure everything was in its proper place for me to slack about. By the time I woke up the next late morning and strolled out onto my porch, I had to remind myself that I'd even moved.

Lunch was as close now as the walk up the hill to Di Island Rum Company patio grill, if I so desired; as was the rum itself. So naturally my semi-daily check-in at the factory was also more convenient. And I'd found out the night before that since my shack was now situated on *exactly* the most westerly point on di island instead of the *almost* most westerly point, I no longer had to turn my head the five or so degrees to watch the sun go down. I was saving time and energy right and left, and all I had to figure out was what to do with it.

But Kaitlyn was arriving on this afternoon, and that gave me plenty of activities for this day, at least. I had everything planned; something I rarely did anymore, but I wanted things to be perfect. I guess

Chester's commitment to Akiko, Marty's reconciliation with Bonnie, and even uncle Billy's booty call had made me long for some companionship of my own. My life was pretty damned good, but perhaps there were ways it could be even better.

When Gus' plane finally taxied up to the southern docks, I was standing ready in my best flowered shirt, with even more flowers in my hand; a bouquet of blue (Kaitlyn's favorite color) plumbagos from Luis' garden, which Geeah had been tending since his passing. And as the Noorduyn's engine shut down I was already hurrying out on the dock to meet her, hoping she would be as brimming with excitement as I was.

Where I met a couple from Wisconsin who were brimming with excitement, instead.

The reason I knew they were from Wisconsin was that they told me so in great detail, right after Gus immediately introduced me to them (I got the feeling he was happy to pass them on to me; being Gus, he didn't care much for chatty passengers). They'd traveled all this way to see the rum factory the Minnesotan owned, and couldn't believe their good fortune in running into him on the dock the moment of their arrival. Which was why they were so very full of excitement, and had so very, very much to say.

It took me a while to get extracted enough from them so I could talk to Gus; they were nice people, but they weren't Kaitlyn, and my flowers were already beginning to wilt in the heat. So after sending them off for a free lunch and rum drink at the factory with John, one of di island kids who liked to meet incoming tourists in hopes of helping them with whatever they needed for some dineros, I jumped on Gus and asked him what was going on.

"Where's Kaitlyn? Did she miss the flight? And if she did, why didn't you wait for her?" I said. "Speak up!"

"What do you mean?" said Gus. "Kaitlyn wasn't on my passenger list today."

"Yes, she was!" I said. "What, did you have too many Painkillers at the Dollar to remember?"

"Hey, I told you a few nights ago that she'd called me to cancel, and that she was going to come over by Roger's shuttle, instead," said Gus.

"Bull," I said. "When was this?"

"On the beach, in Jamaica," said Gus. "You were walking by with that girl, maybe about midnight, and..."

"No, way," I said. "You never said a word to...in Jamaica you say?"

"Yeah," said Gus.

"On the beach?" I said.

"Yes," said Gus.

"When I was with that girl..." I said.

"That's what I said," said Gus.

"Crap," I said.

"What, did you have too many rum drinks to remember?" said Gus.

"It's your fault, anyway!" I said. "You should have known I'd forget."

"*I* remembered," said Gus.

"Yeah, but you're an alcoholic; I'm just an amateur compared to you," I said. "So I suppose that means she's already here on di island somewhere."

"Probably," said Gus. "Way to go, Romeo."

"Any idea where she'd be?" I said.

"Hey, she's your girlfriend," said Gus. "Or was, anyway; if I was her, I'd have hooked up with your uncle by now."

"Thanks a heap; I've got to go find her," I said.

"Luck," said Gus.

I spent the next few hours looking for Kaitlyn; it seemed like no matter where I went and who I talked to, they'd seen her a short time ago but didn't know where she was now. For such a small salty piece of land, it could be devilishly difficult to find someone on di island sometimes. I finally gave up in frustration, and went to think at the secluded lagoon where I'd first taken my Isabella.

And as usually happened when I stopped trying to do something I did it, and found my Kaitlyn there, swimming.

I was surprised how my heart jumped a little at just seeing her, although the view of a pretty woman in a blue green lagoon can easily have that effect on a man. But I had the feeling I would have felt almost the same way seeing her all bundled up in a Minnesota snowstorm, even if I wouldn't have been able to see as much of her. As long as it was Kaitlyn it would have been all that mattered.

She spotted me and waved, a good sign I thought since her greeting used more fingers than just her middle one. And as she walked out of the water, all wet and glistening in the sun, I used my favorite female conversation opener.

"Sorry," I said.

"You forgot, didn't you?" she said, tilting her head in a position somewhere between anger and indifference.

"Yes," I said.

"Jack, Jack, Jack," she said. "What am I going to do with you?"

"Spank me?" I said.

"In your dreams," said Kaitlyn.

"Then I have no idea," I said. "I had this whole day planned; a romantic lunch at Robichaux's, champagne and swimming in this lagoon; a romantic *dinner* at Robichaux's...and I even picked flowers. Their dead carcasses are in my motorcycle's basket over there, so I have proof, even."

"When are you going to get it through that head of yours you don't need to do any of that with me?" said Kaitlyn, reaching out and tapping me on the forehead.

"Maybe I don't need to, but I wanted to; I was an ass about the resort thing," I said.

"Yes, you were, but we already talked about that on the phone and it's long dead," said Kaitlyn.

"I'm glad, but maybe we could still make it to Robichaux's for dinner," I said.

"Or, we could go to that new hut of yours and do something...else," said Kaitlyn, slyly.

"I guess that sounds alright, too," I said.

"On second thought, why don't we just stay right here," said Kaitlyn. "This *is* a lovely spot, and it's perfect weather for a swim."

"That doesn't sound so bad, either," I said. "Except I didn't bring my suit."

"...and that's supposed to be a problem?" said Kaitlyn. "You're on di island, Jack; you've got to learn to relax and just be free."

"I'm workin' on it," I said. "*Always* workin' on it."

And just like that, Kaitlyn and I were Kaitlyn and I, again.

While the best relationships were worth working to keep, there was a fine line before they became simply work. I was lucky, so far; mine and Kaitlyn's was damned lazy, preferring to spend its time enjoying the two of us being together, as opposed to working out *why* we should enjoy being together. Of course, our relationship was still very young, so only time would tell if it would keep its laid back attitude.

But more and more I was thinking I wanted to give it the time for me to find out, for however many years that might take.

Chapter 30
"Island."

There's a celebration I'm joining in today, and it's not something I ever expected to be taking part in, let alone look forward to. But we're all going to be neighbors, and it's time to bury the machete.

Anderton Hotel Properties is throwing a party to commemorate the ground breaking for the Wind Song Resort, with a name and price range I can now live with. It still seemed weird to watch the ceremonial first golden shovel of sand be scooped up roughly were my tiki bar used to sit, but I'm over it and happy to be castawayed where I am now. Happier, actually, now that all is said and done.

I get the feeling it's going to be a bit noisy for a while though, while the property is being built. I'm a fair distance down the sand, but I have my doubts that the quiet rustle of the palm trees and lapping of the ocean waves will be able to totally cancel out the table saws and jackhammers to come. I guess I'll be playing a lot more loud music for a while, so Jimmy and the rest of my island songsters better get tuned up. And if that doesn't do it, I can always keep my own power tool, the Frozen Concoction Maker, revved up into high gear.

I had to give the Anderton boys credit, though; they did know how to throw a party. There was a fine trop rock band playing on risers, a complementary bar, and a buffet table of eats that approximated the menus in their two hotel restaurants to come. And it was only early afternoon; the pig roast and full luau were later in the evening. Which I thought was fittingly ironic, since it was being held where my own so called luaus used to be.

I felt pretty at ease in the midst of my former adversaries, since I'd had a meeting just a few days ago with clipboard and headset; they'd wanted to make sure I was reasonably happy enough with the way things turned out, probably to assure themselves there wouldn't be any crustaceans making there way into the worker's port-a-potties that would soon be arriving on the build site. I told them it was all good, as long as they had no intention of trying to run small places like Monkey Drool's, Robichaux's, the Cantina, and the Coconut Motel out of business. They in turn assured *me* that it should be just the opposite, and that places on di island would have more customers than they knew what to do with. I hope they're right for their sake; they don't want to experience island justice at the hands of Jedidiah (he'll just track them through the jungle, boy, then he'll kick their ass.)

We talked about my rum, too. Or I should say, di island's rum, since even though I own the factory, I still insist it really belongs to di islanders. I had little to do with it, and it is what it is because of people like Luis, Cavin, Faith, Ernesto, and even Billy, who started it way back when; I just sailed in and finished it.

In any case, Anderton wants to feature di rum at their bars and restaurants, and is hoping to work with us in some sort of joint tour deal of the factory. I don't know about that last part; it sounds too organized for my tastes, and I'm not keen on having combined ventures with a corporation. While I've been able to bring myself to reasonably peaceful coexistence, being on the same team would be liable to sour the rum, and my hypocrisy only goes so far. But maybe I'll toss it Cavin and Faith's way and see what they think never the less, since they're the real bosses.

Today though, was all about just having a good time, and finding out exactly what this new resort was about. I had to admit, the table model of the Wind Song looked cool nestled along the fake shore and palm trees, next to the plastic water. Not as cool perhaps as the natural surroundings had been, but I know *I* would have been happy to stay there if I hadn't already occupied the same spot for a couple of years. Hundreds (actually thousands, but that sounds like too many) of people would now be having di island experience, even if it meant di island experience wouldn't be the same as it was *because* they all came. Life was complicated that way, and you had to just pluck the best out of it and toss the rest aside.

As the afternoon wore on and faded into night, di islanders (and quite a few tourists) came and went from the reception. By the time the fire dancers and hula girls started, and the roasted pigs were carried out, my little group of closest friends had congregated into our usual circle. It seemed kind of strange to be celebrating a new Caribbean resort with a Polynesian theme, but that was the tradition at Anderton. The last property they'd built had been in Hawaii, so that decided the party theme for the next one. Which meant that the following resort after the Wind Song would be toasted with a fete based on di island. *That* I'd think about traveling to see; pirates and drooling monkeys and fish gutters; oh my.

My friends and I were all sitting in a circle in the sand around our own private pile of food; Cavin, Faith, Ernesto, Roger, Boyd, and of course, Kaitlyn. I'd talked to Billy earlier in the day to see if he would come, but it was a big no go; he'd said he planned to keep a weather eye on the affair from a distance in case the blaggards tried anything shifty, but that there was no way he'd sit down and feast with them. I felt a little insult to my honor might be in there somewhere for attending myself, but it wasn't the first time Captain Black Dog had chastised me.

I was feeling good and relaxed, and almost relieved. For what was supposed to be a laid back and care free island existence, it seemed like there'd been a lot lately for a worry wart like me to worry too much about. The resort, Marty, Kaitlyn, Luis, the feud between captains Crazy and Black Dog...it was almost as if the stresses of normal life had found me again. And I suppose they had. But at the moment everything seemed perfectly peaceful again, if perhaps somewhat different than before.

"Did you hear they're going to start working on paving the roads next week?" said Ernesto.

"Already?" said Boyd.

"Si; the resort is on one end of di island, and the big docks are on the other end, so they need to start with the roads to move their equipment," said Ernesto.

"That'll make Pat happy, at least," said Boyd. "He's going to start renting out all those bikes he's been having trouble selling, as soon as they have some pavement to roll on. And he says scooters are going to be next."

"Then we should have our first fender bender in no time," I said. "Which means insurance companies will be moving in, followed by the lawyers, followed by more lawyers, followed by-"

Kaitlyn reached out and slapped me lightly on the back of the head, something I'd asked her to do if I started whining about progress again. "Bad, bad, big kahuna!" she said. "What do we say instead?"

"Every little ting is gonna be alright?" I said.

"That's right," said Kaitlyn. "And why?"

"Because it is?" I said.

"Good boy," said Kaitlyn, and she kissed me on the cheek.

We all sat quietly watching the people on the beach for a while; everyone was having a great time at the party, including all the persons we didn't know, who there seemed to be more of than those that we knew. Seeing all these strangers enjoying my island made me finally understand how the true Conchs of Key West must feel, like a bunch of people have camped out in your home and simply won't leave.

"Everyting *is* gonna change now though, isn't it?" said Roger, quietly.

"Yes," I said. "It is indeed. But you know what? That's alright, as long as *we* don't change. They can build and pave whatever they want; I just don't want to ever lose any of you guys."

"We be goin' nowhere, boss," said Faith.

"Yeah, it's still *our* island," said Cavin.

"Maybe we should all get matching tattoos, like star bellied sneetches," said Boyd. "That way we could tell di islanders from the tourists, because they'd all be plain bellied sneetches without stars upon thars."

"Not a bad idea, Dr. Suess," said Kaitlyn.

"I tink I know an even better way to keep di islanders islanders forever," said Roger, leaning forward and motioning us in close. "Listen, everyone; here's what we're gonna do..."

Hours later, at midnight, we stood in a circle on Black Dog's Peak, having been joined by Billy, the Innkeeper, Jedidiah, Mr. Wonbago, Pat, Michel, Henri, and Terrence and Geeah. In our center was a large hole, next to which sat an open wooden chest, filled with talismans. Over the years people on di island had each placed some small thing in the chest to represent themselves, including myself, Gus, and Crazy Chester. If there was a piece of you in there, it meant that you were accepted as an islander.

"Miss Kaitlyn?" said Roger. "Do you want to put something in di chest, too?"

"Me? Oh, no," said Kaitlyn. "Jack told me all about the ceremony and how much it meant to him; I haven't spent enough time here to earn the honor."

"It's gonna be di last chance," said Jedidiah. "If you be tinkin' at all about coming to di island for good..."

Kaitlyn looked at me. "I...don't know. I haven't thought about it yet. So just, go ahead; I understand. But thank you."

"Okay," said Roger, and he straightened himself to his full, short, stocky, height. "In this chest be all di islanders up until today. Tings are changing in our home, and it's time to close and lock di box for good; dat way no matter what happens in di future, all these true islanders will be bound together forever." There was a murmur of agreement, then Roger added, "Does anybody else want to say anyting?"

"Si; I think we should add that we're not locking out any new friends to come; we're just making sure that all di islanders who came before will live in the spirit of di old island forever," said Ernesto.

"Good point, laddie," said Billy.

"Is that it then?" said Boyd.

"I guess so," said Roger.

There didn't seem to be anything else to do, so we simply closed the chest and locked it, then lowered it into the hole and buried it. We didn't put up any kind of a marker; anyone who *should* know it was there *would* know it was there, if they wanted to pay any kind of respects. As for myself, I planned to pour some our finest rum here one day, when it finally was finished aging some years from now. And perhaps save a little bit to drink during the visit.

It was a small thing, Roger's ceremony, but it was the perfect way to move on. And it wasn't meant to be sad, just a nod to passing into a new era, one where you wouldn't know everyone on di island. But as Roger said later, that just meant you could start the day knowing there were many new friends for you to go out and meet.

We sat on the hill and talked, laughed, told stories about one another, and drank rum, and watched the sun rise together. Then we climbed down and said our morning goodbyes and went our separate ways.

But as long as we remained within these shores of Mother Ocean, we would always be together on di island.

Chapter 31
"Let di song of change blow over my head."

I'm lying in the hammock tied between two of my palm trees, Kaitlyn squeezed in next to me. It's morning now, but we're facing the ocean, and between the sight and scent of the turquoise waters, and the tropical sounds softly filling my ears, I have no desire to ever move again in my life.

But I will, of course. There's too much out there waiting for me to see, do, and taste, and too many of my amigos I would miss, no matter how much I love being alone with Kaitlyn. And yes, I'm sure now it's a hearty *"Aye!"* on the big L.

Di island has been steadily evolving in the three months that have passed since our ceremony on Black Dog's Peak. The new paved roads are done, and a sporadic flow of traffic makes its way around them, like the first trickle of electricity must have when *that* modern luxury first came to di island. Right now, it's mostly Anderton vehicles and Hoser Pat's Sporting Goods bicycles and scooters, but occasionally I see a car; like the metallic green, 1963 Chevy Impala ragtop that Ernesto tools around in these days.

And yes, we've had our first fender bender; two, as a matter of fact, the second coming while someone was gawking at the first. But thankfully we don't have a rush hour yet. To be honest, I'm not sure di island is even big enough to have two places far enough apart to to rush between, but you should never underestimate humanity's need to hurry.

Crazy Chester sold his bar and boat stop in the Keys to an enthusiastic buyer from Pittsburgh, who was anxious to escape the cold and hustle and bustle of the big city. But Chester kept the Lazy Lizard, and sailed it to di island to begin taking tourists out charter fishing. He and Akiko purchased Luis' old place, and Akiko is looking forward to putting her green thumb to use in the garden, and the greenhouse she wants to build to provide flowers for places like the Wind Song Resort. And Chester said he would love to someday buy Monkey Drool's, but I wouldn't bet he'll be able to claw it out of the hands of the most interesting innkeeper in the world, so he might have to stick to serving Chesteritas on the Lizard.

My own life has barely changed, despite all my previous worrying to the contrary. If anything, it's even better now. Sure, there's been a couple of days when the construction has gotten on my nerves, but it's been more of an aesthetic problem than anything. I don't want to see a big cement truck parked in the middle of the Crossroads, for example, or yet another rusty freighter full of building supplies sailing towards the northern docks. But I have my quaint little factory and hut to escape to, and as long as that never changes, I'll be able to more than happily survive.

In fact, I had to remind myself that the factory was one of the reasons I needed to get out of my hammock today. The first batch of *Drooling Monkey Coconut Rum* is ready for tasting, and with it comes another excuse to celebrate, and we don't tend to let those pass us by on di island. Even if we humans lived for ten thousand years, life would be too short not to grab all the enjoyment we can. And since on Earth we're lucky to even get a hundred trips around the sun, we better be scooping up those smiles with a trawling net.

So eventually I took all the steps necessary to go to the factory, finishing with the ones taking me and my flip-flops up the hill to it. There on the patio I found my usual unusual band of miscreants, as well as the unusual usual group of newcomers who were slowly becoming a part of di island population. We spent a few moments greeting one another, until the *"KA-BOOM!"* of the cannon, set off by Billy up on Black Dog's Peak, signaled the official start of Coconut Day.

"I'm never going to get used to that," said Chester, who literally jumped a foot off the ground whenever the cannon cleared its throat, and had just set down back on the surface of the planet as usual. If he'd leapt any higher, the ladies might have had quite a view, since he'd dug out his Key West vacation outfit for Coconut Day.

"You might want to avoid standing under di ceiling fans at Robichaux's in di future," said Roger. "Just in case Captain Black Dog decides to make a random announcement."

"And you might want to stay away from the tiki torches today with that grass skirt of yours; we don't need any fire dancers at this get together," I said.

"Did I hear me name a minute ago, mateys?" said Billy, poking his nose in where it belonged.

"Ahoy, Black Dog. Good job on the cannon; right on time," I said, then I thought about it. "Hey, wait a minute; how'd you get down here from the hill so fast?"

"I *am* a ghost, lad," said Billy. "I can do all sorts of things most people can't."

"Nice try," I said. "Fess up."

"Fine," said Billy, irritably. "You know, yer problem, Jacko, and one of the many, is yer no fun. But truth be known, I've been teachin' that new young sea dog, Willie, how to fire me cannon."

I was surprised my uncle would let anyone else clear his gun; he certainly wouldn't let me touch it. Not that I wanted to, since it scared the hell out of me. But I *had* noticed that he seemed to have taken the young man from Cuba under his wing. "So that's what all the random ka-booms have been about," I said. "I was thinking about hunting you down and having a little talk with you about that."

"They weren't random, lad," said Billy. "They were at two o'clock, sharp, and they're gonna be goin' off like that every day now, to let people know what time it is."

"Why two? Why not at noon?" asked Chester.

"I didn't want to wake anyone up," said Billy. "It is di island, after all. Anyway, I figured I better teach someone else how to shoot the thing, since I'm gonna be so busy now."

"Ya, I heard you have an official job, mon," said Roger.

"Aye; I be the captain of this here factory," said Billy, proudly.

"Yeah, I thought Captain Black Dog would be a great mascot to mingle with the guests," I said.

"And I thought I made it clear that if you call me a mascot again, it was gonna be cutlasses at dawn," growled Billy.

"Sorry," I said. "I guess there are wine stewards, so I suppose there's no reason we can't have a rum captain."

"As long as it means I outrank those lily-livered grape drinkers," said Billy.

"That goes without saying," I said. On my ship, rum definitely outranked wine, anyway. And it had more firepower, that was for sure.

"Boss, it's time," said Faith, grabbing my arm and pulling me away. "Everyting's ready."

I followed Faith behind a table by the wall overlooking the ocean (since I didn't have any choice, unless I wanted to lose my arm), and stood between she and Cavin. She whistled sharply to get everyone's attention, and I said, "Welcome, to Coconut Day, everyone!" then waited for the happy applause to die down. "I'm going to keep this short so we can all get down to the important business of enjoying ourselves. I just want to congratulate and thank Cavin, here, for his first rum, and for everything he does at the factory. I know how excited he is, and he should be proud of what he's accomplished in the short time he's been in the business." I picked a coconut cup off the table, and held it up. "And this new rum is named for Monkey Drool's, our favorite place to hang out; thanks for all the good times!"

"You're welcome, mon!" shouted the Innkeeper. "And remember, it be two for ones on all Drooling Monkey rum drinks dis week at Monkey Drool's!" he added, never one to pass up an opportunity to drum up some business.

"Thanks, Franny," I said, never one to pass up the opportunity to use the Innkeeper's given name in front of a large crowd. "Mahalo!" I said, and took a good sized sip of something new, swirling it around in my mouth so all my buds would have a chance to sample it before swallowing.

I waited a few seconds, just to give the moment a sense of drama, then took another sip and did the same routine again.

"It's delicious," I finally said with a smile, which it was.

That was pretty much all there was for me to do. I liked this new coconut rum, and this was my official and brief way of saying it was okay to bottle it and ship it out. Of course, when I say there was nothing more for me to do, I mean aside from drinking more of it, which should pretty much go without saying by now.

I grabbed another cup off the table and brought it over to Kaitlyn, who I'd seen arrive in just the last few minutes during my lengthy speech. "Where have you been?" I said, handing it to her.

"Sleeping," said Kaitlyn. "You know, this island life isn't easy. I don't know how you manage to survive with all the pressures here. Why, just this afternoon, I had to decide whether or not to get out of bed; it was terribly stressful."

"I used to have that same decision making problem back in my old life, too, but for different reasons. I always chose to get up, though. Thinking back now, I wonder why, since I didn't have much to look forward to. I guess it was because I had to," I said. "Here on di island, I have so *much* to look forward to, yet it's hard to get my lazy arse moving sometimes."

"That's because you know there's no rush, since di island isn't going anywhere," said Kaitlyn. "Is it, Jack?"

I looked around me at all my good friends, my lovely little factory, and the blue sky, palms, sandy beach, and ocean that provided the stage for us to sing this island song of ours.

"No, it's not," I said. "Di island is always gonna be here for us. And for anyone else back in civilization who needs to get away to make some rum memories. Life can be so hard; it's a struggle sometimes to remember why we're bothering with the whole thing. But then we go to a place like this, and our senses get filled with something besides TV and Big Macs, and we're reminded of what it feels like to be alive. And we're good to go for another year."

"Unless of course you somehow manage to live like a song *every* day," said Kaitlyn.

"Yes, but that's another story," I said, then readjusted my flip-flops and took another sip of my coconut rum under a tropical sky. "Life can be pretty beachin' if we just give it a chance."

May you find your ass in the water and your toes in the sand, and a big boat drink in your right hand.

Di island, and all di islands living in Mother Nature's care, await you patiently.

Epilogue

Twenty trips around di sun later...

Today is another day of celebration, with yet another party to look forward to. This one is going to be held at my beach shack, although it's hardly a shack these days. But that doesn't stop me from calling it by its old title.

My *shack* is now a two story, three bedroom house, still sitting on the same plot of land beneath the factory. It's island style all the way, with shutters that open big windows to the air, wood floors, ceiling fans, and lots of balconies, patios, and porches poking out in all directions. There may be days that I miss my little old place, but I love this house too, and the reasons for making the change far outweigh my nostalgia for a thatched roof.

You see, I'm married now, and have been for seventeen years. It took Kaitlyn and I three more trips around the sun to commit to permanent ties; not that we were so against it, just that we didn't feel the need. When something's as great as our relationship, you hate to make even the smallest of changes, because you don't want to jinx it. Even by doing something as tiny as, say, getting hitched.

But we eventually and literally took the plunge, with a ceremony held on the beach of my favorite hidden lagoon; followed by a dive by the entire wedding party into Mother Ocean's waters. Needless to say we weren't exactly in tuxes and gowns; they don't mix well with salt water. But tropical shirts and sarongs certainly do.

The big house didn't come until three years later, though, when Billy Jr., my first son, appeared on the horizon. He was named for my uncle of course, Captain Billy Black Dog Danielson, who had died a few months earlier. Billy didn't *pass away*; you don't live a life as full of adventure and harmless, good-natured mayhem as his and then pass away, as if you got bored with it all and decided enough was enough. You die, shouting at the world that you're leaving, like the last rowdy Mardi Gras reveler being tossed out of a Bourbon Street bar; drunk with happiness, and wanting the night to never end.

I wasn't there when Billy departed, but I know how he went; with his usual piratitude. Jolly Roger found him sitting in his Captain's chair on the beached Rum Runner, old Sam by his side, facing the morning sun coming up over the ocean. I imagine Billy plundering a line from my scallywag namesake, Captain Jack Sparrow, and growling it with his last breath; *"Now bring that horizon to me"*. That's how I've written the end of his song anyway, and I defy anyone to challenge the truth of it; they'll be meetin' with the blade of my cutlass if they dare.

When we first became aware that Billy Jr. would eventually join us on Earth to start his own song, we decided it was time to put up a proper home. Everyone else on di island had been doing it, anyway; we were almost the last castaways still keeping it simple. So down came the tiny hut in a tearful ritual that required a hearty rum therapy session afterwards, and up went our new Key West style home. We had to buy a lot of things to fill it, but there's plenty of nearby places to shop for necessities these days.

Di island has grown oh so steadily during my time here. It all started with my little factory, of course. Then the Wind Song Resort moved in, now a classic and well known getaway for singles, couples, and families. After that, new businesses, homes, and islanders seemed to pop up over night. The eastern coast of di island plays host to a vigorous nightlife, anchored by the world famous Monkey Drool's, still owned by the equally famous Innkeeper. Next to which sits Crazy Chester's, home of the renowned Chesterita, owned by, well, some crazy person.

The Crossroads is a bustling tourist shopping mecca now, and I tend to avoid it during the day. But you can also grab a tasty seafood delicacy or boat drink of your choice there at any number of small establishments, like the Cantina. For real food, though,

Robichaux's is still king, with the best gumbo in the Caribbean. That's my five star review, anyway.

We even get cruise ships on di island now; well, one at a time, anyway, since that's all the new docks will accommodate. Those days can truly test your islanditude; three thousand new people at once (and no, they don't get to call themselves islanders, even for the day) hell bent on getting what they want within a six hour window. And woe to those that get in their way.

I sometimes wish Captain Billy Black Dog would appear on the deck of the mighty ghost ship Rumrunner, and send them all down to Davey Jones Locker. Little packs of tourists I've learned to handle, but vast, roving herds of the beasts need to head up to Fantasyland where their kind are welcome. Mickey's more of an equal opportunity host mouse than I'll ever be.

But di island is still di island. Like Key West, it has more charm in its touristy little pinky than any place on Earth. I love it dearly, and like an old friend, I accept its flaws along with all of its virtues.

And speaking of old friends, many of mine are still here, though some have moved on to either other places or planes of existence. Ernesto, Faith, and Cavin remain the pillars of Di Island Rum Factory and Sugar Daddy Plantation, which, although they have both expanded their capacity a couple of times, still do things as old fashioned as common sense allows.

Gus Grizwood finally found the rich broad of his dreams, and lives with her (or off her) in Hawaii. He still flies, but just for fun now. Chester and Akiko never did get married, but they are still talking about it, so you never know. And Chester hasn't donned anything closer to a shirt and shoes in all these years than those coconuts and flippers.

Jedidiah is a well respected artist, who's island prints can be purchased online. Boyd is still Boyd, happy to just make a living how he can and when he can, as long as it doesn't involve steady employment. And Mr. Wonbago left di island for parts unknown, after being defeated in the gubernatorial election three straight times.

As for Jolly Roger, well, he'd be the man that beat him. He's been di island's governor for twelve years now, and it's unlikely that anyone will unseat him while he chooses to run and breathe. They tried to get me to throw my straw hat in the ring for the office when they first decided we needed to put someone in charge, but I said no damned way. The big kahuna was the loftiest title I could ever aspire to, especially since it came with no responsibilities.

And that's how I still like it. Billy Jr., who's birthday we'll be celebrating today at his party, seems far more interested in accomplishing things than I do. He's only turning fourteen, but he already spends hours up at the rum factory after school, learning everything he can from anyone who will teach him. I don't know where he gets it from, but other than having too much drive for his own good, he's a wonderful kid.

My twelve year old son Jack Jr., however, is more like me. Or maybe, more like di island, because he seems to have picked up little personality quirks from certain old friends of mine. It's next to impossible to keep him in a shirt and shoes for any length of time, even when he's playing pirate with Billy's old gear, but he'll happily wear a broad smile no matter what the weather. JJ's already better at playing my old guitar than I ever was, and it's just about the only thing that will keep him in one spot for any length of time, other than napping in a hammock.

But what mini Jack really enjoys is exploring di island. I get the feeling it won't be enough for him when he gets older, though; the walls of his room are covered with maps, and he loves meeting the people that visit here from around the world, and hearing about their homes. I know one day he'll set sail on his own journey to see those places for himself, and find out where his own song truly sings in harmony.

As for me, I've given myself a nickname; Lucky Jack. It helps remind me that while I might have made an effort way back when to try and find a little happiness, mostly it seemed to find me. And maybe that's the most important thing; to do whatever you can to open a path for joy to get to you, because if you let it, life has a way of surrounding you with a wall of shite. And a moat filled with, well, even more shite.

But I've been lucky, as I said. I love my Kaitlyn, for example. It's as simple as that, and that's why I love her. I could go on more, talk about things like how her sideways smile drives me absolutely crazy (in the good way), but that would be like listing the ingredients of a great gumbo. It doesn't matter what's in it; what matters is whether you love it or not. And I love the ingredients that make up my Kaitlyn.

I may be older now, too, but my days aren't that much different than they ever were. True, I don't sit by the ocean and drink rum for nine hours anymore, but that doesn't mean I don't sit by the ocean and drink rum. And you could say I move a little slower, but I'm not sure it's possible to move any slower than I already did when I was younger. I've been on planet Earth long enough that if I were back in the United States, the AARP would have started spamming me with membership letters and e-mails by now, but I don't feel that aged. And besides, I'm not back in the states; I'm on di island, and that makes all the difference in my world.

Here, the days still drift by like notes in a song, continually composing my epic concerto. I don't know if I'll ever find the time to look back and savor all those rum memories I've been storing in my hold, because I keep drinking in new ones. But that's hardly something you'll hear me complain about.

There'll come a time in the not so far away future when the curtain will finally fall on this crazy concert of mine. But I'll play my last note, take my bows with a smile, and sail on. Maybe they'll be an act two, and maybe there won't. That's for the priests and philosophers to think they know, and for me to find out.

I live in my one particular harbor, sheltered from the wind.

I've seen the day when my hair's full of gray, and I know one day, I'll finally disappear.

But not yet.

The end.

CPSIA information can be obtained
at www.ICGtesting.com
Printed in the USA
LVHW011547260420
654464LV00002B/518